Walking Linco

History

with Hugh Marrows

Acknowledgements

In this second volume of Lincolnshire walks my first thanks go to Lincolnshire Newspapers and their parent company Johnston Press. They have been kind enough to both allow me publication space in their papers over the years and now to sanction this book compiled from several years' worth of published articles.

Secondly I must thank my wife for allowing me the time (without too much complaint) to go out and do the walks – though she has done some of them with me. She has then also put up with the hours necessary to undertake the (in some ways) even more time-consuming task of researching and writing up the walks. I must again express my gratitude to my walking companion, of more years than either of us now care to remember, David Cross. David has been on many of these walks with me and very many longer ones too! There are some aerial photographs in this book and for these I must express my grateful thanks to Christina Belton who kindly flew me on a couple of sorties around the county to obtain them.

And finally thanks to all those inn landlords – and landladies – who have kindly given permission for readers to start the walks from their car parks.

Cover image: Rawson's Bridge, Boston.

First Published in 2008 by:
At Heart Ltd
32 Stamford Street
Altrincham
Cheshire
WA14 1EY

in conjunction with:
Lincolnshire Newspapers Ltd
5-6 Church Lane
Boston
Lincolnshire
PE21 6ND

Text and images: ©2008 Hugh Marrows

ISBN: 978-1-84547-187-3

Printed and bound by Ashford Colour Press, Gosport.

I have not attempted an "in depth" commentary on the chosen subjects, any more so than in the original articles from which these walks are taken. This was done partly to avoid long and possibly boring accounts, but also due to the constraints of the space available, particularly when walks include a variety of points of interest all of which deserved some comment. Each walk therefore has one special historical aspect but all feature other items of interest too. Nevertheless we take a wide-ranging, and I hope informative, look at some diverse aspects of our county's history.

Few prehistoric remains survive in Lincolnshire. Although we know that the county was widely settled then, particularly on the higher ground; for example at Nab Hill near Fulletby, the Round Hills near Ingoldsby, Hall Hill near West Keal or at Honington Fort, visible remains are few and far between. They are often inaccessible, as they are on private land, or not close to any public rights of way. And (I'm afraid) what there is to actually see "on the ground" is often something of an anti-climax.

I have been publishing my country walks in Lincolnshire Newspapers now for some eight years and in this second volume it has been suggested that I turn my attention to a selection of routes with an historical theme. This neatly follows from one of my key original aims (apart from encouraging readers out into the wonderful variety of Lincolnshire countryside), which was to try and interest others in our local history, a particular enthusiasm of mine. For me this book is the fruition of a long-held ambition.

The 20 walks I have selected cover both a wide selection of geographic localities throughout Lincolnshire combined with interesting historical places and periods in the region. The walks are presented in historical chronological order. However,

We begin therefore with the Romans, followed by the Vikings before moving on to the Middle Ages. The late 12th century to the early 13th century saw considerable changes in society with a religious culture prompting the founding of many abbeys and priories, of which Lincolnshire has so many, especially in

3

the upper Witham Valley. This period was when the first castle at Bolingbroke was constructed. By the 14th century and 15th century castles were becoming more "domestic" in nature, and status symbols too, rather than fulfilling solely a defensive role; some examples being South Kyme and Tattershall.

Moving on a further two hundred years we find that during the 1700s, the "Canal Age" was at its height, partly as a consequence of the Industrial Revolution. It was then that a number of these features appeared in our countryside only to be followed in the early to mid-1800s with another revolution in transport, and perhaps one of the biggest bringers of social change ever seen in transport systems; the railways. An example of the impact of railways on Lincolnshire people's mobility, for both business and leisure during the Victorian and Edwardian eras, is represented by the growth of the spa resort at Woodhall, which we explore in one of the walks.

Other walks reflect national and international events like World War I and World War II through the inclusion of monuments and memorials along the route. Thus we look at an example of a Lincolnshire link with America and (admittedly a more tenuous connection) with the Battle of Waterloo. Finally at Martin and Metheringham a single walk encompasses the whole spectrum of Lincolnshire history from the Romans to a "Bomber County" World War II airfield.

Some practicalities need mentioning. For walks such as these expensive hiking gear is not really necessary. Use your common sense about clothing; just bear in mind the season and prevailing weather - and remember all these walks are easy half day ones! The exceptions are boots and waterproofs; quality and comfort really are important here! Whilst my route guides and the accompanying maps should get you round these walks without any problems I always counsel having an Ordnance Survey map to hand; if possible make it the relevant Explorer sheet. Drawn to a larger scale they contain much more detail, often useful for interpreting your surroundings over a wider area than we can cover in this book and may be useful in locating the start points more easily. I have used grid references quite a lot in my text and the technique is easily learnt, with each OS map having an explanation and example of this invaluable map reading skill. It is always helpful to know exactly where you are – to plan an alternative route in an emergency, for example. Most walks have an inn or café nearby but carrying a small emergency supply of food and drink is a sensible precaution. On a few walks permissive paths are used; whilst these are identified in the text they will not appear on OS maps!

I hope that in this second volume there is something for all tastes and walking abilities. All the walks have been taken from the original published text but checked and revised where necessary to provide a standard format.

And finally – may I remind readers to obey the Countryside Code! Doing so makes life so much pleasanter not only for others following in your footsteps but for the farmers and landowners on whose goodwill we all rely!

I wish you all Happy Rambling once again!

Hugh Marrows

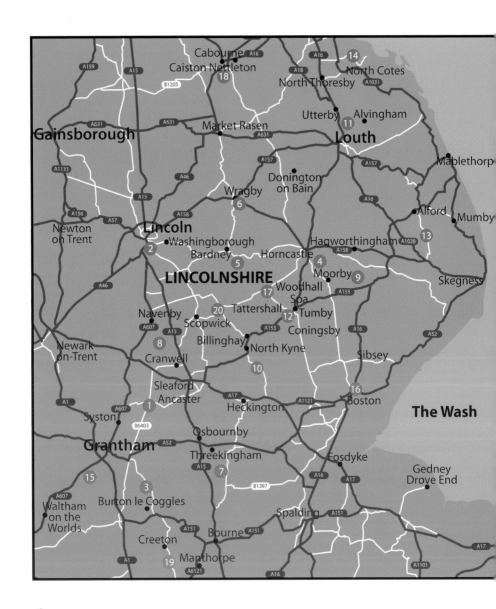

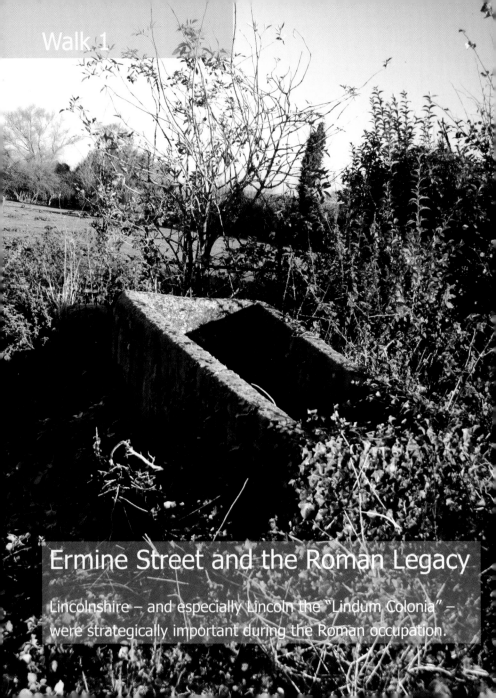

Ermine Street and the Roman Legacy

Lincolnshire – and especially Lincoln the "Lindum Colonia" – were strategically important during the Roman occupation.

The city is well known as the meeting point of two major Roman roads, the Fosse Way and Ermine Street. This short walk takes us round a former Roman camp and along Ancaster's main street, once one of the Romans' vital British road links between London and the north.

A walk around Ancaster provides more than just an opportunity for fresh air and exercise; and of course there is much more of interest than its Roman heritage. The fascinating "Ancaster Trail" also allows us to learn about the area, its geology, and its history – both natural and human.

As a guide I am in a sense redundant here, because information boards are provided enroute, these include route instructions. Nevertheless I shall still offer a few opening comments together with my own brief route description, plus suggestions as to where the trail may be lengthened.

The main street of Ancaster was the Roman Ermine Street (and still bears that name) from London to York. The trail explains the development of Ancaster, the Roman town of Causennae, from its beginnings when it was simply a temporary soldiers' camp, into a substantial civil town. Many important archaeological finds have been made here, including hoards of coins. Indeed Arthur Mee in his Lincolnshire volume of the "*King's England*" series relates that so many coins were found here that in the 18th century locals actually used them as currency. There are also two Roman coffins to see on display in the cemetery.

Between Trail Board 5 and 6 is the Moor Closes nature reserve, which has public access. The sloping ground has a sand and gravel soil with the higher, drier part encouraging a wide range of meadow plants; while the lower area is quite marshy, encouraging an entirely different range of grasses and rushes.

The cemetery across the lane, situated behind the church, has been used since Roman times. It is also famous in botanical circles for being one of only two places in the country where a plant called the Tall Thrift, related to the Sea Pink, grows. (What has always puzzled me is how botanists can be so sure of this!)

Ancaster is an attractive stone built village and the 17th century hall, located near to the church, has an unusual balustrade extending out into the street. The church itself has Roman connections and is built of Ancaster stone. The building is predominantly mid 12th century but stands on a Roman temple site dedicated to St. Martin, who was a Roman soldier before his conversion to Christianity. The church is usually open and inside there is a small exhibition on Roman Ancaster and a detailed local history booklet that is on sale, with all

the proceeds going to the church funds. By the main road, near the church gate, is a Roman statue of "Three Goddesses" found locally; all the "goddesses" are pregnant and represent fertility and prosperity. Opposite the church, Information Board 8 overlooks the site of the Roman township. This is marked on OS maps but cannot be explored directly as it is on private land. The earthworks are nevertheless clearly visible and cover about nine acres. It was at this site that many old coins were found; over 2,000 in one hoard!

NOTES. Two short variations are suggested. The first extends the walk by 1.75 miles; the second by 1.5 miles. The distinctive trail boards bear replica Roman Legion standards and I have put the subjects discussed on them in brackets in the following route guide.

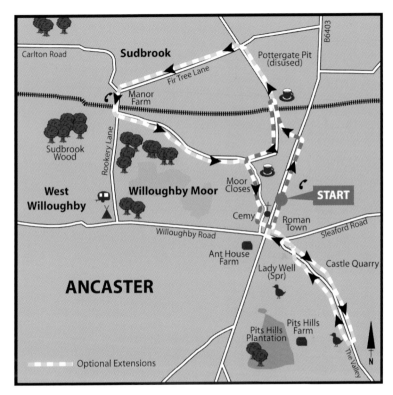

ABOUT THE WALK

START : Ermine Street, Ancaster (near the village hall).

MAPS : OS Landranger 130 (Grantham) : Explorer 247.

DISTANCE : 1.5 miles : 2.5 kilometres.

REFRESHMENTS : Ermine Way Inn, Ermine Street.

1 Board 1 [Roman Ancaster] is found by the village hall. From Board 1 walk north to the school and Board 2 [Roman Pottery] before crossing the road into Water Lane. At the end from Board 3 [Geology] take the footpath to the right leading uphill and cross the railway to Board 4 [Roman Marching Camp].

2 Next retrace your steps to Water Lane but turn right after 250 yards to a path junction and then go left for Board 5 [Ancaster Stone]. Following the same path you will come to the cemetery and

11

Board 6 [Roman Fort and Cemetery], then the church. Go left through the churchyard to Board 7 [Roman Goddesses and Religious Life] on the roadside near the far gate. The final board, Board 8 [The Roman Town] is just across the road, where you can return to the village.

③ Either (or indeed both) of the two short extensions to the walk are worth considering. Neither misses out any of the original trail.

④ The first walk extension starts at Board 4, where you will need to continue north to a lane and turn left for Sudbrooke. There, just south of the

railway, a footpath goes left to rejoin the trail at Board 5.

⑤ For the second option turn left about a 100 yards from the church at the crossroads. This will lead you to the entrance to "The Valley", another nature reserve, but you will need to carefully cross the road to reach it! Just inside the entrance keep to your left as the path rises through trees for about half a mile. After this turn right and descend into the valley, and turn right again to head back towards the entrance.

⑥ The "Ermine Way" inn built in 1898 is in the main street near the start where you can stop for refreshments.

12

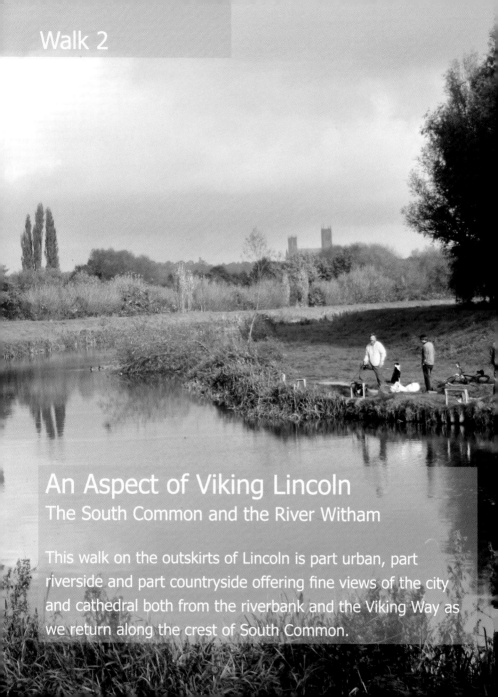

Walk 2

An Aspect of Viking Lincoln
The South Common and the River Witham

This walk on the outskirts of Lincoln is part urban, part riverside and part countryside offering fine views of the city and cathedral both from the riverbank and the Viking Way as we return along the crest of South Common.

The origins of Lincoln's South Common go back over a thousand years to the Danish occupation following the departure of the Romans. As Lincoln's population grew and spread ever further beyond the confines of the Roman walls, extra land was needed to satisfy the grazing rights granted to the freemen. Remarkably these rights remain in existence today: though Lincoln City Council has owned the common since 1915 there is still free access to the site and ponies continue to graze there.

Over the years only small parts of the common have disappeared, firstly when the Lincoln turnpike (now the A15) was constructed and later when the Great Northern Railway line between Lincoln and Grantham was built along the lower edge in 1867. The line closed in November 1965 but its course is still clearly visible near the common and again above Manse Avenue. (GR970680)

The area between the river and South Common has been known as St. Catherine's ever since it was the site of a mediaeval priory. It was there that Queen Eleanor of Castile, wife of Edward I, was embalmed in preparation for her journey to London following her death at nearby Harby in November 1290. Close by the name Cross O' Cliff Hill commemorates the site of the first of the "Eleanor Crosses" that marked her resting places along the way, the final one being Charing Cross in London.

Whilst strolling by the River Witham you may reflect that it has by now flowed about 30 miles from its source near the Lincolnshire/Leicestershire border, which is about 30 miles from the sea. Yet here it is at Lincoln still with 30 miles to go to the Wash! The geological answer to this conundrum goes back to the Ice Ages when rivers such as the Witham and the Trent, which had previously flowed in an easterly direction were deflected to a northerly course by intervening ice caps. When these finally melted the vast amounts of water created cut through the hills to form the "Lincoln Gap", a geographical feature well appreciated from the top of South Common. (You will have learned something of this on Walk 1 at Ancaster!)

Bracebridge was once a distinct village but is now part of Lincoln's suburbia; however its once separate identity is still recalled by All Saints church. Both nave and tower are a mixture of Saxon and Norman work, the tower being 11th century and more Saxon in style, perhaps indicating that it pre-dates the 1066 conquest. If you are lucky enough to see inside there is a Saxon chancel arch and a Norman font. The remainder is Early English but restored in 1875.

NOTES. South Park, Lincoln runs along the bottom of South Common; turn into it off Canwick Hill. There is plenty of parking space. The walk crosses busy roads in places so take care and use pedestrian crossings where available!

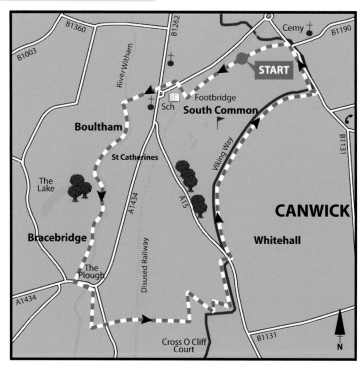

ABOUT THE WALK

START : South Park, Lincoln.

MAPS : OS Landranger 121 (Lincoln) : Explorer 272.

DISTANCE : 4.3 miles : 7 kilometres.

REFRESHMENTS : The Plough or the Waggon and Horses at Bracebridge.

1 First gain access to the common (there are several gates) and turn right along the bottom edge. Ignore the brick road bridge to continue by the fence for 250 yards to a metal pole by a kissing gate and a footbridge. Cross the old railway here, then pass a school (on the left) and walk down to a pedestrian crossing at the road. Cross and turn left.

2 By the roundabout note the Old Police House on the right and at the junction with High Street; go over another pedestrian crossing to walk along Altham Terrace and reach the

River Witham. Now turn left along the riverside path on the far bank. As you walk look back occasionally at the fine views of Lincoln Cathedral. In a mile you will reach The Plough inn on the A1434.

③ To cross the road go right a few yards to a crossing near the Waggon and Horses. On the other side of the road turn left, and once across the river go right on a footpath/cycleway. (Not the grass riverside path!) In about 300 yards, at an open area, immediately turn left between houses and at another road, cross to Manse Avenue beside All Saints church. At the top continue between houses (and over the abandoned railway again) to walk straight up the rising grass path ahead. At a three-way

footpath sign go left for 200 yards to another sign, then bear right uphill. Just as the path begins to swing right look for a footbridge on the left; cross it and turn right, continuing uphill until reaching a footpath sign pointing left. (You are now on the Viking Way.)

4 Follow this path (with fine views!) to join a road. In a few yards turn right to the A15 (the top of Cross O' Cliff Hill)

and cross the road with care, then turn left downhill. Shortly go right through a metal kissing gate onto a secluded, wooded path high above South Common with fantastic views of Lincoln and the cathedral. Eventually descend beside Canwick Hill and near some traffic lights use the metal kissing gate on the left. Cut the corner across the common back to South Park.

The Normans: the next invasion
Boothby Pagnell, Bitchfield and Bassingthorpe

This walk is a pleasant ramble in its own right even without
the main objective of seeing two extraordinary buildings; the
rare Norman house at Boothby Pagnell and the 16th century
manor house in nearby Bassingthorpe.

However the walk holds extra attraction for architecture "buffs" (like yours truly) because of these two extraordinary buildings.

The word "undulating" aptly describes the countryside to the south east of Grantham with its peaceful countryside, rolling hills and the valleys of the East and West Glen rivers. The area has found favour with farmers since prehistoric times with evidence of occupation during the Iron Age supplied by the Round Hills fort at nearby Ingoldsby, (at GR993308 – off route). This countryside was almost certainly occupied by the Romans, as Ermine Street lies only two miles west of Boothby Pagnell.

There is no doubt however that the Normans were at Boothby Pagnell because the Domesday Book mentions it as "Bodebi". The "Pagnell" suffix was added in the 14th century when the manor was held by the Paynell family and near the present hall stands a Norman manor house, described by experts as the "most important" Norman building of its kind in England. It can be seen at close quarters from the walk but is within the private grounds of the hall and viewing is easiest in winter when the surrounding hedges are bare of leaves. Dating from around AD 1200 its windows and doors display obvious features of Norman architecture. The ground floor is made up of cellars and storage space with living accommodation above and

the most notable features is an eight-sided font (15th century), an unusual priest's mass clock scratched into the stonework by the door and the lovely carved angels of the nave roof.

Finally we will visit Bassingthorpe! The surprise here remains quite unexpected from the approach until suddenly both the church and manor house begin to peep over the hillside and then rapidly come fully into view. For once the little mediaeval church (St. Thomas's) is quite eclipsed in interest by the adjacent house. The house dates from 1596 and was built for Thomas Coney, a rich wool merchant. His initials are carved in a panel on the west front with his crest, a rabbit, as a pun upon his name. The house is a riot of decoration with ornate windows, elegant chimneys and stepped gables making it genuinely picturesque from any angle. Bassingthorpe comprises one of the most attractive groups of buildings anywhere in Lincolnshire and particularly so when viewed from the west; so do turn to admire it from time to time as you leave the village.

the remains of the moat can clearly be seen. From the Paynell family inventories it is known that this hall was lived in until around 1596, but by the 1630s a new hall had been built nearby. The present one dates predominantly from 1824.

St. Mary Magdelene's church stands in Lower Bitchfield but the early village that would have been sited around it has since migrated eastwards up the hill. Bitchfield is also mentioned in the Domesday Book and at the church fragments of Saxon masonry suggest an even earlier settlement. Amongst

NOTES. Boothby Pagnell lies on the B1176 and south east of Grantham; park in the lane opposite the church. It is also possible to park at the village hall. Two short sections are on arable land, but one can be avoided.

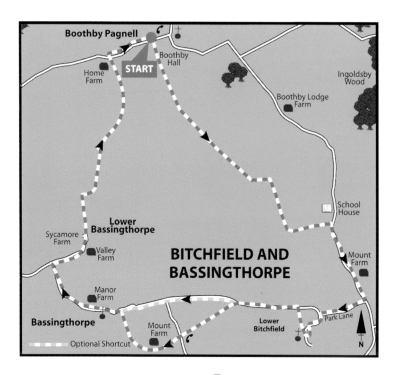

START : Boothby Pagnell village.

MAPS : OS Landranger 130 (Grantham) : Explorer 247.

DISTANCE : 5.3 miles : 8.5 kilometres.

REFRESHMENTS : None on route.

① Walk away from Boothby church to a multi-way footpath sign on the left. Go through the bridle gate and follow the grass track (a permissive bridleway) beside the hall fence to pass the Norman Manor House. Continue for 1¼ miles (approx) to the next sign where the bridleway goes left. Keep moving forward here for a few yards to a waymark by a bend. Ignore the path ahead over an arable field and stay left on the track, going downhill and begin to bear right. When the track veers off through the hedge to the right go left again, now

walk over two arable fields; cross the West Glen River to reach the B1176 road near an old school.

② Turn right, following the pavement into Bitchfield village, passing a pond and the old Crown Inn (regrettably long closed!) to reach a "T" junction. Turn right, re-cross the river and take the next left to reach St. Mary Magdalene church at Lower Bitchfield.

③ By the first churchyard gate there is a footpath sign with a stile a few feet away behind the hedge. From the stile cross a rough meadow, going downhill to a footbridge and another stile. Join a road and turn left. Shortly after a footpath departs leftwards over arable land. (You can continue to Bassingthorpe by road from here if you wish by continuing down

the lane.) Otherwise aim at a hedge gap and tree in line with Westby village (seen ahead) and then cross a second field to emerge at the road, near the Westby village telephone box. Cross onto the lane opposite, which becomes a grass track into a meadow. Bear diagonally right to the far top corner and in the next field walk by the hedge to the road again. Now turn left for the "surprise" approach to Bassingthorpe, with the beautiful manor house and church.

④ Beyond Bassingthorpe village take the first right turn to Lower Bassingthorpe. This "No Through Road" becomes a farm track leading back to Boothby Pagnell. Then when you reach the main road again turn right and head back to the start.

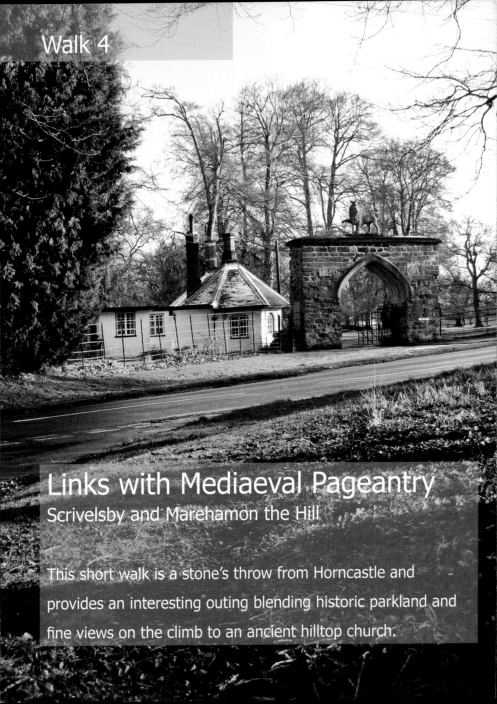

Links with Mediaeval Pageantry

Scrivelsby and Marehamon the Hill

This short walk is a stone's throw from Horncastle and provides an interesting outing blending historic parkland and fine views on the climb to an ancient hilltop church.

The manor at Scrivelsby was given by William the Conqueror to Roger Marmion, whose family had previously been champions to the Dukes of Normandy. Along with the award of Scrivelsby Manor however came the role and obligations of being the Hereditary Grand Champion of England. This is usually abbreviated to "King's – or Queen's – Champion" and the title is the oldest in the land, and unique to this country.

In 1350 the Dymoke family inherited the title through marriage and have retained it to this day. The duties involved riding in full armour into the coronation ceremony on a charger to issue a challenge of mortal combat to anyone who dared defy the monarch's right to the throne. This was done by literally "throwing down the gauntlet"! This full ritual was last performed at the coronation of George IV in 1821 but the Champion is still required to attend coronations bearing a standard. Arthur Mee in his "King's England" (Lincolnshire) observes that there is no record of the Champion's challenge ever being accepted; he also gives a detailed and colourful account of the whole procedure.

Today Scrivelsby Court comprises of just the converted Tudor gatehouse. The first house burnt down in the early 19th century and a replacement was pulled down after World War II. The famous "Lion Gate" beside the road dates from around 1530.

Just down the road a delightful avenue of trees forms the approach to St. Benedict's church. The park is well known for its deer and it is quite common to see them from the public right of way across it. You will certainly see their horizontal browse line on the trees.

Up at Mareham on the Hill the little All Saints church is hidden away behind a farm and can be approached only via a grass path indicated by an imposing signpost. There is a mediaeval chancel but the rebuilt nave dates from 1804. This charming whitewashed building gleams when the sun is on it and although you may find it locked it has clear windows that allow a peep inside to see its blue painted box pews and two decker pulpit dating from the 1780s.

From the open country to the south of Mareham there are views to Lincoln and (on a clear day) to Boston Stump.

NOTES. There is room for considerate roadside parking near the letterbox at Scrivelsby. Part of the way up to Mareham is on a rough headland path before finishing across an arable field. As recompense it is very easy walking all the way back!

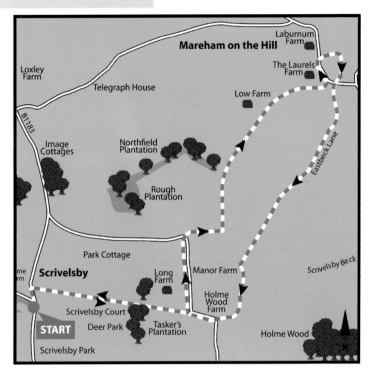

ABOUT THE WALK

START : Scrivelsby (near the Lion Gate).

MAPS : OS Landranger 122 (Skegness) : Explorer 273.

DISTANCE : 4.3 miles : 7 kilometres.

REFRESHMENTS : None on route.

1 From the letterbox cross the road and turn left to reach a footpath sign near a gate and cattle grid. Turn right and enter the park heading towards Scrivelsby Court and in 50 yards or so, as the drive bears right towards the Court, keep to the left and walk onto the grass track.

2 Keep walking forward until you reach a kissing gate at the corner of some woods. Walk alongside the woods and when you pass a second kissing gate keep moving directly ahead, walk over

the deer park to a third kissing gate in the deer fence at the far side. Pass through some trees to a field gate and then walk across rough pasture to join with a lane. In a few yards at a junction turn left walking past a farm and descend towards the ford at Scrivelsby Beck. (There is a footbridge!)

③ When the lane bends left turn right onto a short, signed track and then walk ahead across an arable field. At the far side turn left and walk uphill, keeping the hedge to your left. Near the top of this large field veer slightly right to cut the corner, looking for a waymark in a hedge gap in front of you. Now continue with the hedge to your right eventually

passing between it and a copse near the ruins of Low Farm.

4 A few yards further on and the path goes through the hedge, so that the path is once more on your left. From the next hedge corner go across a final arable field aiming just to the right of the end house where a footpath sign stands by the road. (Or follow any path marked in crops; this may not take a direct line.)

5 When you reach the road turn left and walk towards the direction sign for the church, at this sign turn right and

walk up the grassy lane to a small hand gate for access to the church. Return to this gate and veer left through some trees, however, when you reach the track do not set off across the field ahead. Instead bear right to emerge at the road, almost opposite another track.

6 Cross onto the track and head downhill, keep walking ahead where the track forks. In a little over a mile you will meet a surfaced road. Keep walking forward to rejoin the outward route, there you will be able to return to the start by re-crossing Scrivelsby Park.

Twelfth Century Monastic Life
Southrey Wood and Tupholme Abbey

Our primary feature of interest here is Tupholme Abbey, though there are many other attractions for walkers along the way.

The railway through Southrey was built in October 1848 for the Great Northern Railway Company. Known locally as the "Loop Line" it was the main line from London to the north until the more direct Peterborough, Grantham and Doncaster line (the "Towns Line") opened in 1852. The Loop Line was a busy goods line conveying agricultural produce, and popular for "Fisherman's Specials" as it closely followed the River Witham between Boston to Lincoln. Southrey

Station remained operative until the line closed completely in October 1970. However, the old platform still proudly bears its name board and there are fine riverscape views from it.

Just up the road, in complete contrast to most Lincolnshire village churches stands the delightful St. Johns, so reminiscent of American "New England" colonial style buildings. It was built entirely of wood in 1898 by the village carpenter Richard

Turner, helped by the vicar, curate and villagers – and the cost – £130! The external appearance has been faithfully preserved even though it was clad in PVC in 1987. Inside the font and altar rail are from Navenby and the reredos came from St. Georges Hospital chapel in Lincoln.

To the northwest of the village there is a moat site (at GR133671 and just off our route) that marks the location of Seney Place, an outpost of Bardney Abbey, once used as a sort of mediaeval convalescent home. The ground rises slightly here and had formed a low island before the marshes were drained. These features gave Southrey its name, the "south" part referring to its geographical relationship to Bardney Abbey. Further north are Southrey Woods, part of the Bardney Limewoods Nature Reserve, with permissive footpaths that are especially attractive in springtime.

The marshy Witham Valley appealed strongly to the mediaeval monastic communities, for it offered isolation but with a river providing transport and communication, and for these reasons a string of nine abbeys grew up within as many miles. One of these was at Tupholme, the "sheep island"; "Tup" is a Saxon word for sheep still in use today. The Abbey was founded around AD 1155 by a small group of "white" monks from the Premonstratensian Order (an Order originally founded in France).

The Abbey was always a small establishment with only two dozen or so monks living there. In the 1536 the Abbey was suppressed during Henry VIII's dissolution of the monasteries but an unusual remaining feature that was not destroyed is the stone pulpit set high in the refectory wall. A nearby moat surrounds what was the site of the original wooden church. Following the Dissolution some of the Abbey stone was used to build a mansion for the Willoughby family but this was later demolished and replaced by a farm (which was also later demolished in the 1980s). There are information boards placed around the site that describe the monk's daily life and the Abbey's history.

Extraordinary as it may seem now Tupholme Abbey was the site of a huge pop festival in 1972 starring Rod Stewart and the Beach Boys.

NOTES. There is free parking at Southrey Station. Two shorter walk alternatives (not described in detail) follow the entire Southrey Wood permissive path, returning along the Viking Way (from GR125684); or return to Southrey by road from the far side of the woods. Both of these miss out Tupholme of course. Both Tupholme Abbey and the riverbank offer good picnic spots.

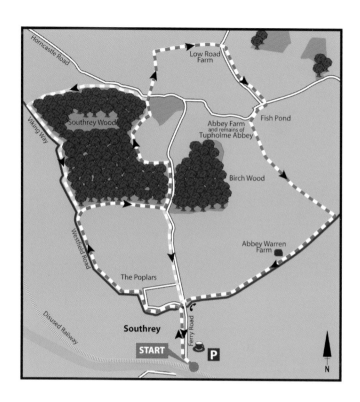

ABOUT THE WALK

START : Southrey old station. (GR139663)

MAPS : OS Landranger 121 (Lincoln) : Explorer 273.

DISTANCE : 5.3 miles : 8.5 kilometres.

REFRESHMENTS : Riverside Inn, Southrey.

① Walk into Southrey Village along Ferry Road and turn left when you reach the Viking Way at High Thorpe Road. Follow this road as it bends right, turn left at the next junction onto Westfield Road and then walk along a farm road to a footpath sign. Just beyond this is another sign for the permissive footpath within Southrey Wood.

② In the woods follow the clear path on the right leading to the road at the far side of the wood. Bear left here, parallel to the road, but staying within

the woods until the path eventually veers away from the road again. Stay on the path inside the woods going round three sides of an open field until the path splits. Take the narrower right hand branch and at a house join a public footpath.

3 Bear left, leaving the woods to cross Horncastle Road onto a continuing path on the other side. When level with some warehouses take the path on the right. After a footbridge bear right slightly to a stile next to where a farm drive meets a lane. Turn right again and at the B1190 road turn right for a few yards before turning left into the grounds of Tupholme Abbey.

4 A clear bridleway passes the Abbey but you should take time to explore before continuing along the bridleway to a surfaced lane near Warren Farm to meet the Viking Way again. Turn right and keep walking forward across the meadows in front of the farm onto a green lane that leads to a bridge over Tupholme Beck. A clear (though perhaps muddy) track now leads back to Southrey. Turn left to head back to the start of the walk.

Birthplace of a Mediaeval Statesman

Wragby and Langton by Wragby

This simple "there and back" walk starts from Wragby Market Place to visit the birthplace of Archbishop Stephen Langton who, apart from the king, was once the most powerful man in the kingdom.

Wragby is an ancient town and 350 years ago it had three annual fairs plus a weekly market, even though the royal charter of 1668 that authorized them was never approved by Charles II. Near the start we pass Turnor Square, a group of almshouses (1840) and All Saints church (1839) built of yellow brick. We will also pass the impressive earthworks of an old mediaeval, moated manor house where there was once a mortuary chapel.

On the way to Langton we cross the former Louth to Bardney railway line which opened in 1876 and finally closed in February 1960 when goods trains ceased.

We reach Langton at its history information board; a fascinating read! To appreciate the age of the surrounding landscape look into the field behind the board and you will see the mediaeval "ridge and furrow" field pattern is still there, whilst across the lane are earthworks of the mediaeval village and the moat of the manor house.

Down the lane is Langton church, dedicated to St. Giles, the patron saint of cripples and beggars. The tower is the oldest part and has large pieces of fossilised seashell embedded in the masonry surrounding the west door. Note too the metal memorial arch over the gate erected for Edward VII's coronation in 1902.

Stephen Langton was born in this remote village around 1165 to Henry Langton and from humble beginnings became a biblical scholar and ecclesiastical politician. He rose through the church to become Archbishop of Canterbury in 1207. He was the first to arrange the books of the Bible into the chapters that we recognize today and was principally responsible in 1215 both for drafting the Magna Carta and organizing its

signing by King John at Runnymede. A surviving copy of the Magna Carta is on public exhibition at Lincoln Castle. Bishop Langton died in 1228 and is buried at Canterbury Cathedral.

NOTES. An alternative return route from Langton is offered. This adds 1¾ miles and covers some rougher ground. (See route instructions.)

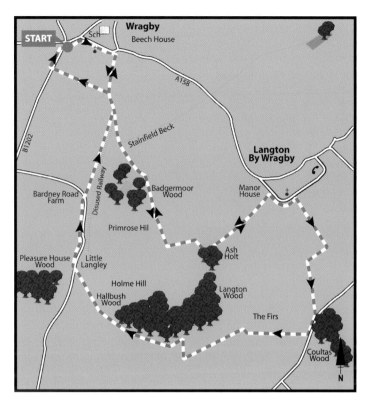

ABOUT THE WALK

START : Wragby Market Place.

MAPS : OS Landranger 121 (Lincoln) : Explorer 273.

DISTANCE : 4 or 5.6 miles : 6.5 or 9 kilometres.

REFRESHMENTS : Inns, café and chip shop in Wragby.

1 From the traffic lights in the Market Place turn right (towards Louth/ Horncastle) and right again at the road junction. Beyond the church and old school make a third right turn onto Cemetery Road. Keep walking along this track past the cemetery and from a three-way footpath sign continue over the grass towards a footbridge in the hedge. Cross this and in 25 yards bear left over another footbridge and then you will walk over the old railway until you reach a kissing gate. From the gate

41

bear right and walk towards a stile in the far corner of the meadow and continue uphill past Badgermoor Woods (on your right).

2 From a footbridge near a barn in the field corner walk through trees to a farm road. Keep ahead and in 100 yards go left at a waymark having a hedge on your right. At the hedge end turn right over an arable field to another waymark within the trees of Ash Holt. Now turn

left, leaving the woods along a grass track to a road. (Langton's village history board is to your left.) Turn right to reach the church.

③ [Return the same way to the three-way fingerpost by the cemetery. Then follow the instructions in the the final paragraph of the longer route (*)]

④ For the longer route climb the stile opposite the church gate and cross a paddock to a second stile. At the next field (arable) the path splits; take either branch, but the left hand one along a wide grass strip is easier. In the second field bear right along a grass track and at the field corner you will rejoin the other path. (Avoiding the arable field in this way is, for 100 yards, not strictly a right of way. The farmer would probably prefer that we didn't walk on his crops; if asked blame the author!) Now bear left along a good headland to a road.

⑤ Turn right and in 150 yards go right again at a footpath sign along a field headland and at the corner enter a farmyard via a stile. Walk straight through to another stile where a grass track begins and shortly climb two more stiles on your right, then turn left by a hedge onto another track aiming for the barn ahead. Join a farm road, turn right and just beyond some electricity wires turn left on a track by woods keeping ahead past a derelict cottage (datestone 1850) and continuing downhill to a footbridge. Cross this and turn right by a beck to a bridge, then go left on a track. At a fence corner (the old railway again) climb a stile and walk diagonally over a paddock to a stile and a road.

⑥ Using the verges where possible bear right for a quarter of a mile until, just after the entrance to "Primrose Hill", you see footpath signs on the right. Use the right hand path, nearest a fence and the beck. This path will eventually rejoin the outward route; where you must return to the fingerpost near the cemetery.

(*) Now turn left towards Wragby Mill passing moats and earthworks to reach a kissing gate. Walk through a housing estate towards the main road and turn right, walking back into the Market Place.

Home Grown Monasticism in the 10th Century

Pointon and Sempringham

This walk, set in the south of the county, visits the site of an early mediaeval priory established by a deformed monk, which was the only monastic order to be founded in England.

St. Andrew's church Sempringham is the church at the end of a track over the fields but we begin our walk in Pointon.

St. Gilbert of Sempringham was born around 1083 and was the son of a wealthy Norman knight. However, he was badly deformed and because of this was deemed unfit to train in the knightly pursuits that would normally have been his role in life as a nobleman's son. Nevertheless as a young man he was able to travel to Paris for an education and on his return obtained the post of secretary to Bishop Alexander of Lincoln.

St. Gilbert harboured a desire to found a religious organisation but he initially established a local school. Then, in 1131, with the blessing of the bishop and the King he founded his own monastic order – to become known as the Gilbertines – and built St. Mary's Priory at Sempringham. The Gilbertine Order was unique for being the only Order to admit both men and women. The men and women of the Order lived separated lives either side of a dividing wall with the Priory church itself similarly divided.

The Order remained an exclusively English one and became relatively successful in Gilbert's lifetime. By the time of his death in 1189 (at the reputed age of 106) there were thirteen priories throughout the land, housing 700 monks and 1,700 nuns.

The Sempringham Priory was destroyed during Henry VIII's dissolution in 1538

and the land bestowed upon Lord Clinton (later the Earl of Lincoln) who re-used the stone to build his own mansion on the site. The mansion has now gone but faint earthworks remain to the south of the church. Sempringham Village lay to the northwest of the present church and it too has entirely disappeared though the church, now St. Andrew's, which has much Norman stonework, is still there. On the church's south wall is a memorial to St. Gilbert and below it a three dimensional map shows the position of the Priory, Lord Clinton's mansion and the village. The OS map also indicates the site of monastic fishponds to the southwest of the Priory. At the bottom of the churchyard, by the hedge, you will also find a Holy Well.

At the bottom of the track below the church is a monument to Gwenllian, a Welsh princess imprisoned at Sempringham for 54 years, almost her entire life in fact, until her death in 1337.

Back in Pointon the village pump, outside the school, commemorates Queen Victoria's Diamond Jubilee in 1897 and in Pinfold Lane opposite is the unusual black and white tin Christ church built in 1893.

NOTES. Considerate parking is also possible nearby in West Road, Pointon.

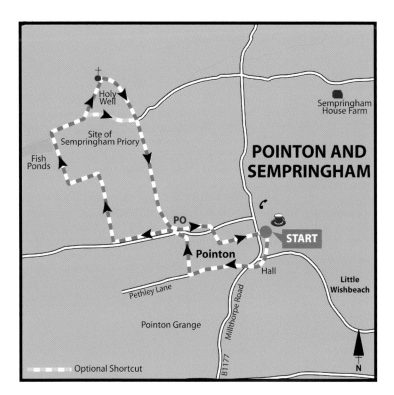

ABOUT THE WALK

START : Old Ship Inn, Pointon.

MAPS : OS Landranger 130 (Grantham) : Explorer 248.

DISTANCE : 3.3 miles : 5.25 kilometres.

REFRESHMENTS : Old Ship Inn, Pointon.

1 From the Old Ship Inn car park cross the road and turn left. Walk along the main road, continue round a right hand bend and then bear right onto Pethley Lane. At the junction with Pinfold Lane keep walking forward for 200 yards until you reach two footpath signs pointing right. Take the nearer footpath with a ditch on your left. At a road turn left and walk out of the village to reach a signed track on the right and some 200 yards beyond the last house.

2 Follow this path uphill, through two bends and down to a sleeper bridge over the Marse Dyke. Turn right again here

until you are level with a footbridge on the right. A diagonal field path now goes off to the left and comes out alongside the churchyard hedge.

3 Enter the churchyard at a stile and leave by the far gate. A track now descends to the Gwenllian memorial by the Marse Dyke. (Alternatively, if the field is muddy, continue by the Dyke to the Gwenllian memorial and walk up to the church from there – returning the same way.)

Cross the Marse Dyke by the bridge and proceed onto the grass footpath rising in front of you. Follow this over the hilltop and down the far side to a footbridge across a stream. In the field beyond bear half left to a small gate by a house; the village Post Office.

4 Turn left along the road and turn right at Pinfold Lane opposite the school. Just round the corner beyond the church a footpath/alleyway on the left leads back to the main road and the Old Ship Inn.

A Knights Templar Estate
Temple Bruer

This short walk over level, easy terrain explores the historic landscape around Temple Bruer. It is suitable for all ages, and young children will probably enjoy exploring the preceptory tower at Temple Farm.

We start at a junction of ancient trackways across the Lincoln Heath, an area once the haunt of highwaymen and so remote that for centuries travelers needed the services of local guides. So inhospitable was it that in 1751 local landowner Sir Francis Dashwood erected an inland lighthouse, the Dunston Pillar, which still stands beside the modern A15.

We begin our walk at the little church of St. John, which is quite new as churches go, having been built as recently as 1874. The church was designed by James Fowler the famous Louth architect who was also responsible for restoring (or rebuilding) many of Lincolnshire's churches. It looks quite stark with its rugged stonework, but there are attractive lancet windows and a little wooden bell tower. In the lane alongside is a plaque relating to local history.

We set off along Warren Lane, which as its name implies, was the site of the rabbit warrens for the Temple Bruer preceptory. In the Middle Ages rabbits were "farmed", both for food and fur, in controlled warrens enclosed within limestone walls. There were so many here that the area became known as the "Rabbit Republic".

A preceptory was a large farming estate with a church, owned and managed by the Knights Templars who were an association of knights and fighting monks

formed after the 12th century Crusades. Their original role was to protect pilgrims visiting the Holy Land and also to defend the area from invasion by Saracens. The Templars' original base was at Solomon's Temple in Jerusalem, hence the derivation of their "Templar" name. Their aims, gallantry and religious zeal soon became legendary and attracted benefactions from monarchs and noblemen throughout Europe. The Templars became, in time, an extremely wealthy and influential organisation, founding many large religious-farming estates on land given to them.

The preceptory at Temple Bruer was founded in the early 12th century. Other similar sites in Lincolnshire are known at Aslackby and Willoughton. "Bruer", the second part of the name, derives from the French word for heath, "bruyere". The present remains are of the southeast tower that was once connected to a circular church, copying in its design the Church of the Holy Sepulchre. The tower enjoys free access and there are detailed information boards at the site. Within the tower there is a lot of carved graffiti, some dates being several hundreds of years old. You might try a family competition to see who can find the earliest! (Let the author know if you can beat 1689.)

Nearby Ermine Street pre-dates Temple Bruer by over a thousand years, being the primary Roman road link between

London and York. Entering Lincolnshire at Stamford it ran through the Roman city of Lincoln to reach a ferry at Winteringham on the Humber. The large mosaic passed on the extended walk is by Arik Halfon and it too reflects various aspects of local history, the mosaic style itself recalling the Romans artistic tastes.

NOTES. An optional extension (to 4½ miles) follows part of the famous Ermine Street Roman road. There is ample parking at the start which is situated on a minor road west of the A15, about seven miles north of Sleaford. For refreshments you must continue to Wellingore (2½ miles away) where there are two pubs.

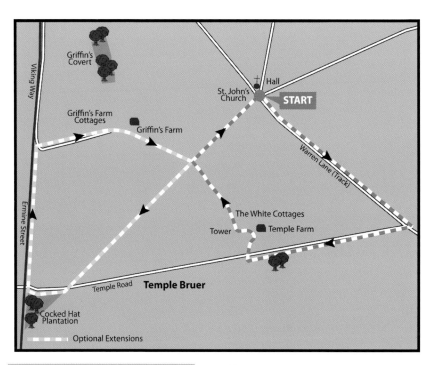

ABOUT THE WALK

START : St. John's church, Temple Bruer. (GR010547)

MAPS : OS Landranger 121 (Lincoln) : Explorer 272.

DISTANCE : 2.5 miles : 4 kilometres.

REFRESHMENTS : None on route.

1 From the church cross to Warren Lane, the green lane immediately opposite, and follow this to a road and at this junction turn right. The shallow valley to your left as you approach Temple Bruer was the site of the now vanished mediaeval village linked to the preceptory. In three-quarters of a mile turn right again into the farmyard at Temple Farm. At the back of the farmyard, behind the buildings is the preceptory tower of the Knights Templars. Take a break for an exploration and to study the various information boards.

② When you are ready to continue, leave the farmyard by the track in the back left hand corner. In a quarter of a mile you will reach a track junction. Here you can make a final right turn and walk back to the start.

③ The extended route however turns left along a green lane. Follow this to a road, bear right for 300 yards and then go right again, northwards now along Ermine Street (part of the Viking Way). When the "Street" becomes surfaced,

near the mosaic pillar, bear right to Griffins Farm, continuing until you meet the track left earlier. Now turn left and return to the start of the walk at St. John's church.

Birthplace of a Plantagenet King
Old Bolingbroke and West Keal

This energetic walk from the birthplace of King Henry IV also features one of Lincolnshire's finest views. Much of it is on country lanes so it is a good winter walk; however, there are still short field sections along the way.

Old Bolingbroke village lies hidden in the Wolds about three miles west of Spilsby and was mentioned in the Domesday Book of 1086. First records of a castle here date from around 1230 but by the 14th century it had come into the possession of one of England's most powerful noblemen, John of Gaunt, Duke of Lancaster, whose son Henry was born here in 1367. Following his banishment by Richard II, Henry returned to England to head an uprising in 1399. Henry was accepted by Parliament and crowned Henry IV in 1399; he reigned until 1413.

Geoffrey Chaucer was a frequent visitor no doubt because he was related to Katherine Swynford through marriage,

being the husband of her sister Philippa. Katherine had been John's mistress for many years, a situation that prevailed throughout his two previous marriages, but after his second wife died he finally married her at Lincoln in January 1396.

The castle was damaged and then looted for stone following the nearby Battle of Winceby in 1643. By the 1960s the ruins had become just mounds covered in turf; what we see today has been excavated and revealed since then.

The plan is quite intriguing with six lengths of twelve-feet thick walls that connected five round towers and a gatehouse that faced the church. There

coast. St. Helen's church is built of local "green" sandstone and dates mainly from the 12th and 13th centuries. In the churchyard are the four large stone pinnacles, remnants of the earlier tower that fell down in 1881 and was rebuilt by 1884.

On the return to Old Bolingbroke you will see Hall Hill on your left. This spur of high, open ground was once a prehistoric settlement and 6,000-year-old flint implements were found here during excavations in the 1930s. Further excavations in 1956 established that occupation of the site had continued until Anglo-Saxon times.

are several information boards within the castle grounds explaining the layout of the castle, how it would have looked and discussing the lives of those living there. In the village itself John of Gaunt built a large church but the one that survives now is much reduced in size. The south aisle remains the only part of the original building and has become today's nave, leaving the tower in an unusual offset position. The Red Rose of Lancaster was adopted in 1280 and was based upon the "Provins" variety. Today some of this same species (presented by the town of Provins near Paris) grow in the flowerbed where our walk starts.

West Keal churchyard commands perhaps the finest vantage point in southern Lincolnshire. The village is seen far below and on a clear day the view encompasses the Wash and Norfolk

NOTES. Park by Old Bolingbroke church (near the village information board) and look for the rose bed and village sign as the walk starts from here. This is a good walk for picnickers. West Keal offers an outstanding vantage point or use the grounds of Old Bolingbroke castle. A short section is over arable land. The inn at Old Bolingbroke does not open every lunchtime and you should try to call ahead to see if they are serving lunch. (Tel: (01790) 763 388 for opening times.)

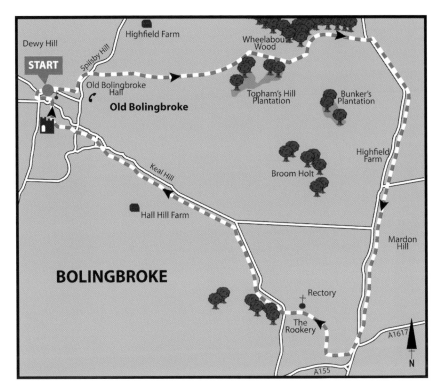

ABOUT THE WALK

START : Old Bolingbroke village.

MAPS : OS Landranger 122 (Skegness) : Explorer 273.

DISTANCE : 4.3 miles : 7 kilometres.

REFRESHMENTS : The Black Horse, Old Bolingbroke.

① Set off past the churchyard, pausing to look inside the gate, at what appears to be a stone gatepost. Actually this "gatepost" is the gravestone of a local carpenter who wanted a memorial representing his occupation to stand in the grounds.

② Continue to the junction with the road leading to the village of Mavis Enderby (Spilsby Hill Road) and turn left. In 250 yards climb the stile on the right to follow an ancient lane uphill.

3 From the stile at the top of the lane proceed straight across the next field (where the lane has been ploughed out) to rejoin it at a gate in the fence. Follow this green lane until you have to cross an arable field ahead to a hedge corner, then keep forward so that the hedge is on your left. When the hedge itself bends off to the left, turn half right, descending to a footpath signpost. Continue downhill to cross a footbridge and a stream, then climb uphill to join a track; turn left along this until you reach a road.

4 Turn right now walking for a mile (and ignoring two junctions) before dropping steeply to the A16 road. Turn right and continue for 50 yards (using the pavement) and then climb a stile on your right. Staying near the bottom of the field walk to a stile in the far corner near a barn. From the stile go through the farmyard to a lane and turn right uphill for 200 yards. Bear left at the top of the lane and go over a field to another stile, go over the stile and then through a kissing gate into West Keal churchyard. By now you have earned that picnic!

5 To continue the walk follow the lane from the church for 150 yards to a road and turn right. In about half a mile at the

next junction bear left downhill into Old Bolingbroke. When the road forks, keep right and you will reach a "T" junction; there turn right and immediately left for the castle. At a small access gate enter the castle grounds, explore and finally exit near the church. Bear left to return to the start of the walk.

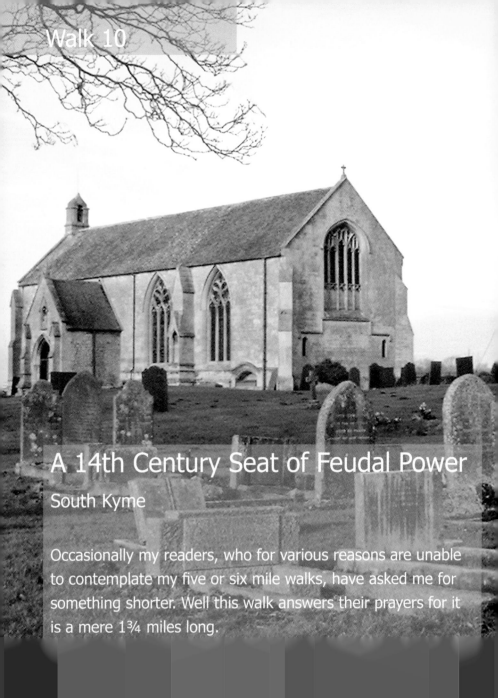

A 14th Century Seat of Feudal Power

South Kyme

Occasionally my readers, who for various reasons are unable to contemplate my five or six mile walks, have asked me for something shorter. Well this walk answers their prayers for it is a mere 1¾ miles long.

South Kyme is the only village beside the River Slea throughout its course between Sleaford and the River Witham at Chapel Hill. The Slea's lower reaches were known for centuries as the Kyme Eau, indeed the name has survived onto 21st century OS maps. The village originally developed on one of the few patches of raised ground amongst what was then undrained fens (see how it is centred above the five metre contour on modern maps) and on what is today the site of the present day church and Manor House. The earliest inhabitants were probably the Celtic Coritani tribe, who also had a settlement at Old Sleaford,

probably followed by the Romans who built the nearby Car Dyke that linked the Nene in Cambridgeshire to the Witham at Lincoln.

South Kyme's recorded history begins around 1100 and the village assumed considerable importance once the de Kyme family had become lords of the manor, "Barons of Kyme" and Sheriffs of Lincolnshire. Around 1170 Philip de Kyme founded a small Augustinian priory (the monks wore black robes and were called the Black Canons) where St. Mary's church now stands. Enlarged by Simon de Kyme, and later by the

Tailboys family, the priory survived until the Dissolution in 1536.

In the 14th century the manor passed to the de Umfraville family and around 1340 Gilbert de Umfraville proceeded to build a fortified house here of which today's Kyme Tower is the sole remains. That house in turn was demolished (except the tower of course) around 1725 and the present manor house was built by re-using the stone. Earthworks still remain south of the church both for the original manor house moat and the gardens of the 18th century house. After finishing his new house Gilbert de Umfraville went on to enlarge St. Mary's church and the priory. Although fragments of the early masonry remain, the church was much reduced following the Dissolution and again during rebuilding in 1805. However, in 1890 a new chancel was added.

The walk partly follows the Kyme Eau, which for centuries before the building of the Sleaford Navigation had been navigable to a point some 2.5 miles west of South Kyme. We know that the navigable "Eau" had existed since at least 1343 for in that year Gilbert de Umfraville petitioned King Edward III for the personal right to charge tolls in order to pay for embanking and maintenance. We know too that building materials for Tattershall Castle, begun in 1434, were transported along the "Eau".

Amongst all this history some modern artwork is to be seen too. Between the High Street and the Navigation stands a large wooden carving of a kingfisher by Simon Todd and near the start is an ornamental archway commemorating the 1994 bicentenary of the opening of the Sleaford Navigation.

The suggested extension to the walk follows the Kyme Eau northwest to Ferry Bridge. This is known locally as "Ha'penny Hatch". One explanation of this name is that the "halfpenny" referred to was the passenger charge when there was a ferry here, and later a toll bridge. Another version is that local children received a halfpenny to lie on boatloads of hay, flattening it sufficiently to prevent it catching against the bridge – and also at Town Bridge in South Kyme. Near Ferry Bridge the Navigation is conspicuously straight where it uses a short section of the Roman Car Dyke.

NOTES. The walk starts from a small parking area just north Bottom Bridge, beside the Sleaford Navigation bicentenary memorial. The terrain is easy and the extension to Ferry Bridge adds a further 2.5 miles.

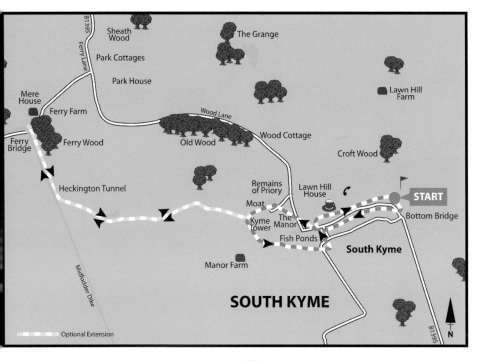

ABOUT THE WALK

START : South Kyme at GR178498.

MAPS : OS Landranger 130 (Grantham) : Explorer 261.

DISTANCE : 1.9 miles : 3 kilometres.

REFRESHMENTS : The Hume Arms, South Kyme.

1 We will begin our walk at Cross Bottom Bridge and turn right onto the sign-posted footpath beside the navigation (you'll see the kingfisher sculpture on far bank from this section) and continue to the road at Town Bridge. Turn right over this, join High Street and cross to the pavement opposite. Turn left. Just after the road bends right cross again (with care!) to a footpath sign by twin kissing gates and take the partly surfaced field path towards St. Mary and All Saints church. You will there join a lane at a second pair of kissing gates opposite an entrance to the churchyard.

Walk 10

Turn left past the church and the Kyme Tower to reach a bridge over the Navigation.

2 [For the extended walk cross the bridge and turn right. A good grass path leads to Ferry Bridge and along the way there are distant views towards Asgarby and Ewerby churches on the skyline. From Ferry Bridge return the same way.]

3 After crossing the bridge turn left beside the Navigation and walk back to Town Bridge. Here you may choose between keeping ahead and retracing the outward route or return along High Street for a closer inspection of the kingfisher sculpture.

14th Century Upheavals in Rural Life
Fotherby and Brackenborough

Brackenborough is one of Lincolnshire's best-preserved "lost" mediaeval villages. There is open access to the village so it is a wonderful site to explore.

We begin at Fotherby where lining the main street are six fine almshouses built in 1867 to a design by James Fowler of Louth. They were paid for by Everitt Allenby, born locally at Manor Farm in 1794 and who "made good" as a businessman in London. When he died in 1863 his will also paid for a new chancel to St. Mary's church. This is just round the corner and is also a James Fowler design that replaced the demolished mediaeval church; the date can be found on the drainheads. The striking brickwork interior is a characteristic of Fowler's work.

The lost village site of Brackenborough has open access under the DEFRA Countryside Stewardship Scheme and is one of the county's most extensive, with house plots and streets being extremely clear. So why has it all gone? The early 14th century suffered from persistent bad weather for many years resulting in meagre crops. There were changes in agricultural practices with much arable land being taken over for sheep, meaning that fewer farm workers were needed. Those remaining were poor, undernourished and in no condition to face the onslaught of the Black Death that occurred in 1347–48. Rural populations plummeted and in Lincolnshire alone we know of over 200 villages disappearing. They did not all go at once of course, nor do we know which of these factors applied to Brackenborough or their precise impact.

In fact the Black Death may not have been too devastating for in 1086, when the Domesday Book was prepared, there were roughly 16 people living at Brackenborough but this rose to about 28 by 1377. All had however gone by 1565. The hall dates from the early 18th century though there would have been an earlier manor house here, something indicated by its surviving moat.

The beautiful Little Grimsby Hall was built around 1700 for the Nelthorpe family. The tiny whitewashed St. Edith's church dates from 1500 according to a plaque near the west door and stands within the hall grounds, though there is public access.

Returning along the former railway track it is difficult now to visualise this as the Grimsby to London main line. When opened in 1848 it was the first route built by the Great Northern Railway and it was not until 1939 that some stations were closed. But it was in the 1960s that decline really set in with final closure coming in October 1970. It is nice to see some track and Fotherby's old level crossing gates preserved!

NOTES. There is room for considerate parking in Fotherby's main street. As there are often animals grazing in Brackenborough Park ensure that dogs are kept on leads. For refreshments the Brackenborough Arms is a mile away towards Louth.

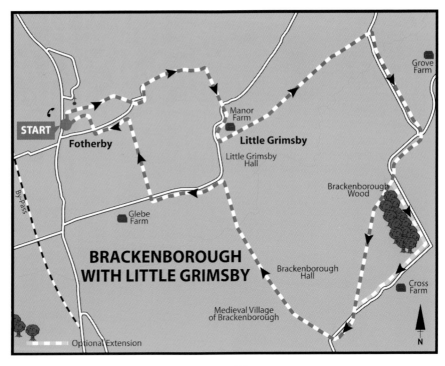

ABOUT THE WALK

START : Fotherby village.

MAPS : OS Landranger 113 (Grimsby) : Explorer 282.

DISTANCE : 6.2 miles : 10 kilometres.

REFRESHMENTS : None on route.

① Set off walking down Church Lane (from the corner by the almshouses). At the end keep ahead on a footpath to a kissing gate then go down long meadow to another kissing gate at the far end on the right. Beyond this, on the old railway, briefly bear right then walk left between hedges to a lane.

② At the lane turn left until a farm track begins; then take the footpath on your right beside the woods. At the next track turn right to reach a road and then go right again. After a double bend look

for a signed bridleway on the left. (It may be concealed but it is next to a post box).

③ In almost a mile you reach a road, turn right and right again at a junction. Beyond a bend a footpath goes off to the right beside woods. At their corner bear half left towards a waymark in a hedge gap maintaining the line across two more fields to a road. Turn right and in 250 yards go right again along the approach avenue to Brackenborough Hall. (If the fields are muddy you can simply stay on the road!) As you proceed you will pass the DMV; an access map is near the estate entrance.

④ After exploring continue your walk towards the hall, go over a cattle grid and up the house drive. By the coach house bear right, then left along a gravel drive to a cottage (there's a waymark on the garage) and left through trees. Next walk downhill by a post and wire fence to a gate, turn left over a footbridge by a ford and follow a track to join a road at a bend. Turn left. (But see the next paragraph first!)

⑤ Little Grimsby church is in the hall grounds. To visit the church walk forward along the road for a few yards to a small gate in the fence on the left. Cross the footbridge just inside and walk behind

the hedge round to the church. When you are ready return to the road and rejoin the main route.

6 From the bend follow the road for 500 yards to the old railway bridge. Just before it go through the hedge gap on the left and down to the trackbed before turning right under the bridge and continuing to the old level crossing near Fotherby.

7 Turn left for 250 yards then go right into a farmyard. Keep to the right of the house where two kissing gates lead into Church Lane. Turn left to head back to the start.

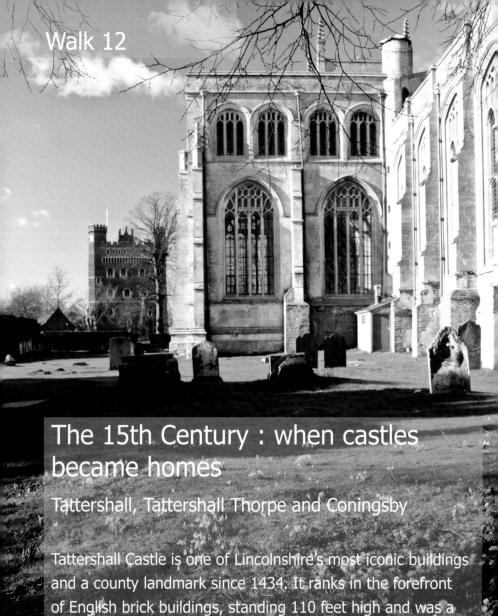

Walk 12

The 15th Century : when castles became homes

Tattershall, Tattershall Thorpe and Coningsby

Tattershall Castle is one of Lincolnshire's most iconic buildings and a county landmark since 1434. It ranks in the forefront of English brick buildings, standing 110 feet high and was a colossal undertaking for the 15th century.

Contemporary accounts record that some 320,000 bricks were used to complete the dungeons alone! Its owner (and perhaps designer) was Ralph Cromwell Treasurer of England to Henry VI and an extremely wealthy man. However by the beginning of the 20th century it was internally derelict and was purchased by Lord Curzon of Keddleston in 1911, who restored it and upon his death in 1925 passed it to the National Trust. (There is an admission charge at the Castle for non-members of the National Trust.)

Nearby is Holy Trinity church, founded in 1438, its splendour again emphasising the wealth and status of its patron and builder; Cromwell again of course! It took thirty years to build and was finally completed fourteen years after his death in 1455. Nearby are the charming Bede Houses; the present ones date from the early 16th century and are successors to Cromwell's original almshouses of 1440.

Nearer to the Market Place is Tattershall College, the remains of Cromwell's college of priests, founded to administer his church and possibly as a village schoolroom. In the Market Place itself there is a mediaeval cross and a more recent addition of an intriguing millennium sundial.

Lying between the college and the church is a short length of the Horncastle Canal largely formed by "canalising" the River Bain. The canal left the river

here heading for the Witham, hence this abandoned, detached section. The canal scheme was strongly supported by Sir Joseph Banks and building began in 1796 but not until 1802 was it fully open into Horncastle. The progress and success of the railways finally forced its closure in 1878.

Away from Tattershall we stroll through Tattershall Carr Woods owned by the Woodland Trust, a national charity with over 1,100 woods in its care throughout the country. The Trust encourages freedom to roam for visitors. Here you will see the remains of several obvious military-style buildings that once formed part of Thorpe Camp. RAF Woodall opened in February 1942 as a satellite base for RAF Coningsby. The main airfield lay to the north of Tattershall Thorpe but the site spilled over the Coningsby to Woodhall road. Thorpe Camp was built with mess and NAAFI facilities along with various shelters and stores. Following their spectacular raid on the Ruhr dams, 617 Squadron (the Dambusters) came to Woodhall and from here flew their mission to sink the Tirpitz. The main part of Thorpe Camp (off route) is now a visitor centre with an English Electric "Lightning" fighter aircraft parked by the entrance.

Our walk also crosses the Great Northern Railway's "New Line" which ran from Stixwould Junction to Bellwater Junction near Firsby. This was the last main line

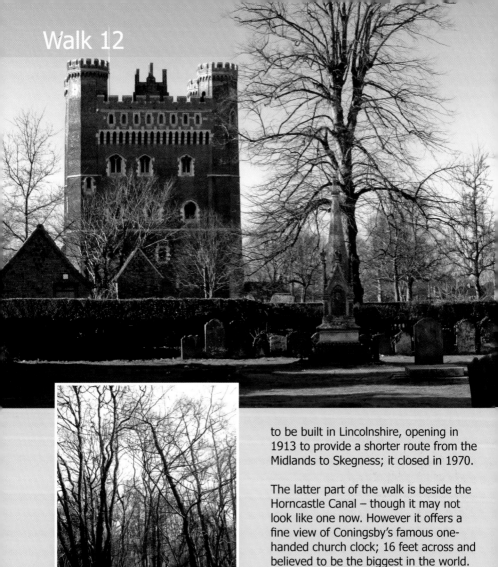

to be built in Lincolnshire, opening in 1913 to provide a shorter route from the Midlands to Skegness; it closed in 1970.

The latter part of the walk is beside the Horncastle Canal – though it may not look like one now. However it offers a fine view of Coningsby's famous one-handed church clock; 16 feet across and believed to be the biggest in the world.

NOTES. On leaving Tattershall a short section of road walking is unavoidable. Please take care until you reach Lodge Farm.

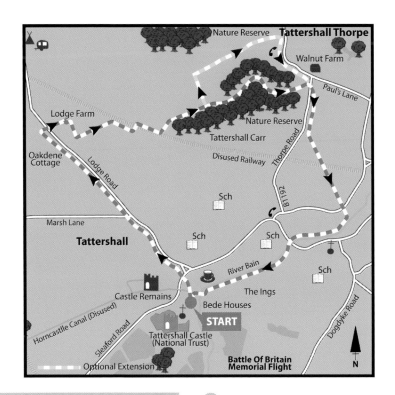

ABOUT THE WALK

START : Car park at Tattershall Castle.

MAPS : OS Landranger 122 (Skegness) : Explorer 261.

DISTANCE : 5.3 miles : 8.5 kilometres.

REFRESHMENTS : Fortescue Arms and there is also a Chip Shop in Tattershall. Blue Bell, Tattershall Thorpe.

PICNICS : Tattershall Carr Woods.

1 From the car park walk away from the church to the old canal and cross the nearby footbridge onto a fenced path leading into the Market Place. The "College" buildings are now just to your right. After visiting them cross the road, walk through the Market Place to leave Tattershall via Lodge Road. When the pavement ends continue walking about ten minutes until you reach Lodge Farm.

2 Turn right at the footpath sign immediately after the farm, then go right again behind the last barn to a waymark on an electricity pole at the field corner. Now go left along a grass headland. At the next corner bear right to reach

right at the first fingerpost; this track leads straight to the inn. You should then turn right through the village to rejoin the main walk.]

③ The main route enters the woods at the footbridge, turn left on a clear path within the trees and not long after go right, then left, to reach the exit at a road; cross the road carefully to the pavement opposite. [Alternatively you can reach the Blue Bell from here by turning left but return to this point.] Otherwise turn right and in 300 yards take the signed footpath on your left heading over a field towards the old railway embankment. Climb up and over this to cross another field to a hedge corner and reach a road. Take the footpath opposite and continue walking to the canal/ River Bain.

④ Turn right through a metal kissing gate to follow the riverbank to a road, then cross both the road and the bridge before continuing by the river – on the opposite bank to where you started. On reaching a weir cross the footbridge into the car park where you began.

another footpath sign and a footbridge. Cross the footbridge and turn right by trees to a stile and cut across the corner of an arable field (only a few yards) to the edge of Tattershall Carr Woods. Keep walking forward, with the trees on your right side, to reach a footbridge. [Visit the Blue Bell by turning left and then

Links with America
Willoughby

Lincolnshire's famous adventurer Captain John Smith was remembered in 2007 both here and in the USA as celebrations marked the 400th anniversary of the founding of Jamestown and the American colonies.

This walk is my contribution to Anglo-American relations and explores the countryside around Smith's birthplace at Willoughby.

John Smith led a swashbuckling life that reads like something from a "Boy's Own" adventure. Born and baptised at Willoughby in 1579 he was then educated at Alford Grammar School, at that time situated in the room above St. Wilfred's church porch. He next attended Louth Grammar School before taking an apprenticeship in King's Lynn. The monotonous life there held no appeal and aged nineteen he left to become a mercenary soldier fighting the Spanish in Holland, and later taking on the Turks in Eastern Europe. There his luck ran out for he was captured and enslaved but eventually escaped back to England via Russia. In December 1606, he learned of the founding of the Virginia Company. He forthwith set sail for America with the first expedition sent

to establish a colony there, arriving in Chesapeake Bay in May 1607, where the settlement of Jamestown (named after James I) was built. Within two years Smith was elected as president.

Even there his restless spirit drove him to explore and map the interior and write of his travels. It was during this time that his association with Pocahontas the Indian "princess" arose. Captured by Powhatan Indians, Smith was sentenced to death until Pocahontas (then aged eleven) begged her chieftain father to spare his life. She afterwards visited him in Jamestown until such time as Smith returned to England in 1609. Smith was back in America five years later, naming "New England" and identifying Plymouth (the Pilgrim Fathers eventual destination) as suitable for settlement. He and Pocahontas did meet once again in 1616 when she arrived in England as the wife of Norfolk settler John Rolfe. When Captain John Smith died in 1631 he was buried in Newgate cemetery, London only to have his gravesite lost in the Great Fire of 1666.

The Willoughby Arms has a portrait of Smith on the outside and inside memorabilia includes a bell from the God Speed, one of the Jamestown expedition ships.

Walkers should visit Willoughby's St. Helena's church too. On one side of the south door is a commemorative plaque to Smith donated by the Jamestown Foundation and on the other a colourful memorial window. This shows scenes from Smith's life and his coat of arms incorporating three Turks heads, recalling those he had killed in single-handed combat. A village history information board stands beside the lane between the church and the inn.

The walk also follows part of the former branch line from Willoughby to Sutton-on-Sea. This was opened in 1886 by the Sutton and Willoughby Railway Company (S&WRC) but was worked by the Great Northern Railway, who eventually took over the S&WRC in 1908. Goods services ceased in 1964 and the last passenger train ran on October 5, 1970. The section near Willoughby is now a nature reserve with public access and acts as a haven for wild flowers and numerous species of butterflies.

NOTES. Between Willoughby and Bonthorpe some arable fields are unavoidable; dry conditions are therefore preferable.

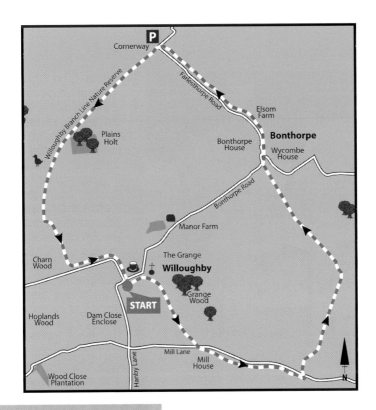

ABOUT THE WALK

START : Willoughby Arms, Willoughby.

MAPS : OS Landranger 122 (Skegness) : Explorer 274.

DISTANCE : 5 miles : 8 kilometres.

REFRESHMENTS : The Willoughby Arms. (Alternatively you could picnic beside the railway.)

1 From the inn car park turn right to reach the church and a footpath signpost by the churchyard gate; enter and turn right. (Note the path is paved with old gravestones!) At the moat around the rectory turn left onto a footbridge. Cross this and cut across the garden corner to a stile by a gate. Once over the stile walk across the meadow to another stile in the far hedge. Maintain this direction in the next field aiming for the right hand corner of trees at the far side. Cross the footbridge there onto a track. At this point the path divides.

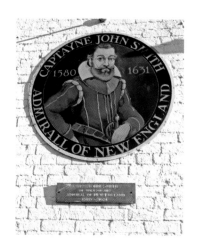

2 Take the right hand branch to meet a road, turn left and in half a mile turn left again at a signed track. Walk down this for about 150 yards to a footbridge on the right. (You may reach this point over the fields if you wish and if conditions underfoot are fair. To do this bear half-left where the path divides, cross a footbridge and maintain a more or less straight line to reach the track and footbridge mentioned above.) Either route will bring you to the point where you cross the footbridge by the track and then on the opposite side continue to walk half-left to a group of

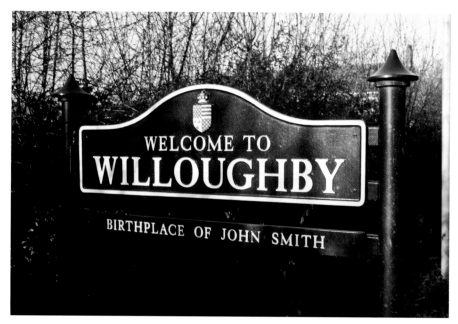

trees. From the next fingerpost aim for the right-hand end of the trees seen on the horizon and you will eventually reach another fingerpost and footbridge near an electricity pole. Do not cross this bridge but bear left veering slightly away from a ditch and aiming left of centre of more woods in the distance.

3 On joining a track keep walking forward for 200 yards until the track bends right. From a signpost leave the track maintaining a line (very) slightly left to what you have been walking. The path should be marked in any crops and will lead you to another footbridge and a road.

4 Turn right when you reach the road, keep walking ahead at the nearby "T" junction and continue through the hamlet of Bonthorpe. In about a mile, where the road bends sharply to the right, turn left through a gate onto the old railway line.

5 In another mile when you reach a gate bear left a few yards until you come to a track and go right along the track to a road. Now turn left back into Willoughby. At a bend cross the road onto the village green and continue walking over the green towards the Willoughby Arms.

The Canal Age
Tetney Lock and the Louth Canal

The Louth Navigation, the earliest of Lincolnshire's major canals, opened in 1770 and preceded both the Sleaford Navigation (1794) and the Grantham Canal (1797). The canal took seven years to build and it cost £28,000 (a considerable sum in those days) even though costs were minimised by the flat nature of the marsh landscape.

Of the seven locks required, six were in the last three miles between Alvingham and Louth, the other being the final sea lock at Tetney Lock.

The Louth Navigation is unique amongst Lincolnshire canals because from the outset it was built on an imaginative scale, with wider and bigger locks to allow seagoing vessels to reach Louth. This strategy considerably enhanced its trading capacity whilst simultaneously lowering costs by avoiding the transfer of goods from ship to canal barge. The Navigation rapidly prospered, and remarkably because of silting problems at Grimsby, became the more important fish dock for a time. Technological

progress, first in the form of railways and then road transport, began to affect the canal's profitability. What finally sealed the Navigation's fate was the devastation caused at Louth Riverhead by the disastrous Louth Flood on May 29, 1920; the Navigation Company simply could not afford to repair the damage. One of Navigation's original warehouses still survives at Thoresby Bridge.

The Tetney Blow Wells (grouped around GR32006) are managed as a nature reserve by the Lincolnshire Trust and are only glimpsed from this walk. (There is public access however and a waymarked walk within the reserve; a map and route description may be downloaded from www.lincstrust.org.uk) In local legend the wells are said to be bottomless and to have engulfed horses and carts without trace, but investigations in the 1960s found them to be no more than sixteen feet deep. Their proper description is "artesian springs", that is water under pressure being forced from underlying rocks through overlying layers; in this case from chalk about 65 feet down through a covering of glacial clay. The chalk strata extends inland to the Wolds and heavy rainfall there will dramatically increase pressure causing a surge at Tetney after two to three months, but it has been estimated that on average any particular drop of rain takes between two and three years to complete the journey.

Those interested in old churches might like to make the short detour to St. Peter and St. Paul's (GR317009) which is a fine old 14th century building in the perpendicular style. One north aisle pillar records building work in 1363, though the chancel is from the Victorian era.

NOTES. The Explorer map omits (literally) just a few yards near Tetney village. Don't worry about this – the missing bit is shown on sheet 284 if you really want it!

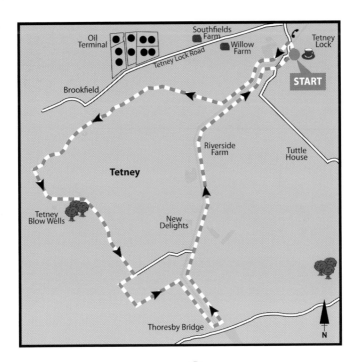

ABOUT THE WALK

START : Crown and Anchor Inn, Tetney Lock (GR343022).

MAPS : OS Landranger 113 (Grimsby) : Explorer map 283.

DISTANCE : 5.6 miles : 9 kilometres.

REFRESHMENTS : Crown and Anchor Inn, Tetney Lock. The Plough and a chip shop are off route in Tetney Village.

1 Cross the bridge in front of the inn and turn left down a short lane to a stile, continuing along the canal bank to a bridge. From there follow the track to the right for three-quarters of a mile (ignoring another path branching right) until a wide bridge at a lane junction is reached.

2 Cross the bridge and take the narrow enclosed path opposite that runs beside a scrapyard, which leads into a large meadow. You should now head for the meadow's far left-hand corner and cross a double stile and footbridge near a dilapidated barn. Keep to the left-hand edge of a garden, cross another stile and join an unsurfaced lane. Turn right and walk to the road junction of Church Lane

and Hoop End, continue going forward another 150 yards to a footpath sign pointing left. (Continue ahead if you wish to visit Tetney church and village.)

3 The footpath runs between hedges into a meadow. Stay by the right-hand hedge to a stile in the corner before crossing the Tetney Drain footbridge and

4 Otherwise bear left to another footbridge and walk beside the trees surrounding the reserve to a stile. (Between the two is a gate and a stile. To get a clear view of Well No 4 climb the stile and turn left inside the boundary hedge; return the same way.) Continue to yet another footbridge from which you will bear right, still by the woodlands surrounding the Blow Wells. At the corner the path continues forward running alongside a dyke. Follow the waymarks until you reach a track; from it the path continues a few paces to your right, and with the hedge on your right. From another footbridge climb an embankment and turn right, staying on the top through two left turns to reach the canal.

5 Turn right to reach Thoresby Bridge and cross it to the opposite bank. Then turn left along the path below the concrete wall and the old canal warehouse. Simply following the canal for two miles returns you to Tetney Lock and the Crown and Anchor Inn.

another footbridge just to your left below the far bank. (Here you can detour into the Tetney Blow Wells reserve if you wish; look to your right to see a pumping station – walk past it to pick up the path. You will emerge at the gate mentioned in instruction 4.)

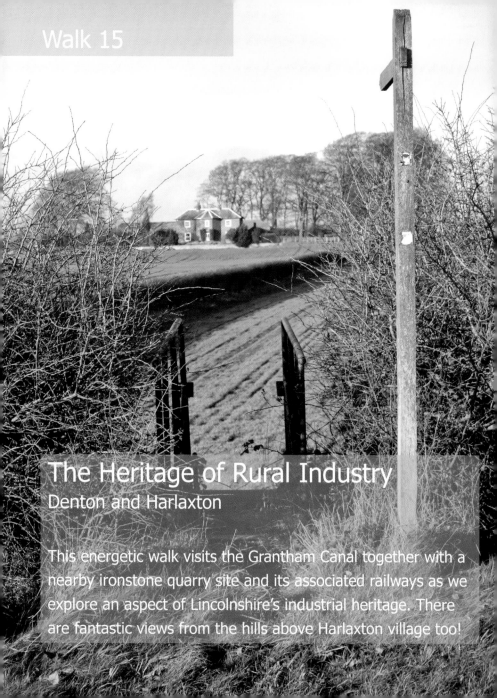

The Heritage of Rural Industry
Denton and Harlaxton

This energetic walk visits the Grantham Canal together with a nearby ironstone quarry site and its associated railways as we explore an aspect of Lincolnshire's industrial heritage. There are fantastic views from the hills above Harlaxton village too!

From about 1770 Nottingham became the hub of a new canal and river transport system as the growth of large urban populations coincided with advances in agriculture that created marketable crop surpluses in towns like Grantham. City factory products needed trading for the farmer's produce. Grantham Corporation realised this need and began to plan for a canal between the town and the River Trent. An authorising Act of Parliament was obtained in 1793 and the canal was completed by 1797.

Our walk passes close to Harlaxton Bridge, the village's canal wharf (now long gone) which was sited in the impressive Harlaxton Cut. This 20-feet-deep, mile long cutting heading towards Grantham, was one of the major civil engineering works of the whole 33 mile canal. Nearby was another, the massive Denton Reservoir (also visited) built to feed the canal with water. Covering 27 acres and with a capacity of 61 million gallons it is now a popular fishing venue.

The hills surrounding Harlaxton are composed of vast strata of Jurassic ironstone rocks stretching southwards to Northamptonshire and within Lincolnshire these became extensively quarried where the ore was easily accessible around Denton and Harlaxton. Quarrying had first taken place near Woolsthorpe, with the ore being removed by canal barge, but this restricted production so much that in 1883 the GNR built a branch line to Woolsthorpe Wharf. The need for further increased production soon saw this extended beyond Denton and up Swine Hill near Harlaxton to reach larger quarries at Stroxton; the railways climb being achieved by switchbacks still marked on modern OS maps. Our walk offers glimpses of these old railway lines as we cross the tracks twice near Denton and at the switchback sites southwest of Harlaxton.

Changing economic conditions and competition from the railways forced the canal's decline and final closure in 1929, whilst the cessation of ironstone mining resulted from cheaper foreign imports and brought about the abandonment of the ironstone railways in 1974.

The charm and appeal of Denton and Harlaxton villages stems from the local geology too for they are built from the same golden-coloured ironstone. St. Andrews church at Denton is mostly 13th century and close by is a delightful Queen Anne style house, the former village school. At Harlaxton Lincolnshire's famous architectural extravaganza, Harlaxton Manor, can be seen. It was designed by Anthony Salvin and built for George de Ligne Gregory between 1831 and 1837. (The best view is from the Gregory Arms car park.)

NOTES. Park considerably in Denton; there are spaces near the school and the inn.

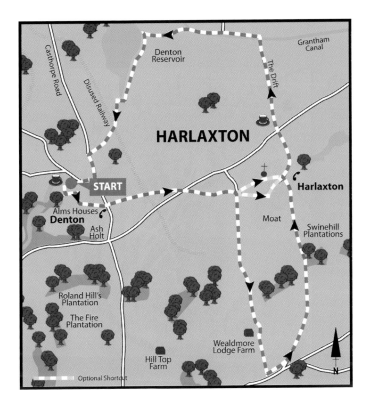

ABOUT THE WALK

START : Denton village, near Welby Arms.

MAPS : OS Landranger 130 (Grantham): Explorer 247.

DISTANCE : 5.6 miles : 9 kilometres.

REFRESHMENTS : The Welby Arms, Denton. The Gregory Arms, Harlaxton.

1 Walk past the front of the inn and the churchyard before bearing left on a signed path along the old school drive. From a kissing gate keep ahead across part of Denton Park to a lane and turn right. Go left from the footpath sign at the lane end, over more parkland, then between cottages to a road. The path continues opposite between more cottages into a large meadow.

2 Now bear slightly right, look for the spire of Harlaxton church on the skyline and aim at that. Briefly losing

sight of the church cross an old railway line to maintain your direction uphill over an arable field. At the A607 the path continues opposite over a field to join a lane into Harlaxton and reaches a junction with Rectory Lane.

③ (A short cut here saves two miles. Take the road into the village or the footpath opposite that leads to the churchyard, where, at the far end another path leads to the road again. Both options reach the war memorial; then see 5 below).

④ The main route however takes the footpath from the field gate to your right over a rough meadow to a stile, then over an arable field to a second stile. Now comes a steep climb up through meadows (where the railway switchbacks ran) to Wealdmore Lodge on the hilltop. Keep left of the farm walking between trees to its access road. Continue walking ahead along the edge of a large, flat field created by iron ore removal, the scale of operations revealed by a metal ladder in

the corner; climb this to reach the road. Turn left and left again, descending into Harlaxton village once more. (From the war memorial visit the church along the footpath behind the cottage across the road to your left.)

⑤ Otherwise bear right through the village to the main road (A607) and the Gregory Arms. Cross the road carefully into a lane called "The Drift" and walk downhill to the canal. The site of Harlaxton Wharf and Cut are seen from the bridge but the walk takes the footpath to the left immediately before it.

⑥ In a quarter of a mile the canal veers away to the right. Ignore the bridleway to your left, keeping directly ahead, first over a stile and then along field edges and over footbridges to finally reach the reservoir embankment. Turn left and cross the feeder stream at a footbridge. Turn left beside the stream, crossing the abandoned railway line once more, to reach a road. Turn left and finally walk back into Denton village.

Changing the Face of the Fens
Boston and the Witham Navigable Drains

This short walk is on the doorstep for Bostonians! To the north of the town the Witham Navigable Drains extend for over 40 miles in total and are for much of their length accessible to boaters from the River Witham via Anton's Gowt.

Some two miles to the east of the Anton's Gowt lock is Cowbridge where several of these drains meet in what might be described as Lincolnshire's (certainly Boston's) "Little Venice".

The huge areas of the East and West Fens presented drainage problems for millennia and efforts to tame them go back centuries, the first recorded efforts being in 1532 and with the Maud Foster at "Cow Brygge" being mentioned in 1568. The Maud Foster was possibly also improved as part of further attempts at local drainage undertaken by Sir Anthony Thomas in the 1630s. (He gave his name to "Anton's" Gowt). However, an estimated 40,000 acres of fen were still regularly flooded, a situation which resulted in John Rennie being asked in 1797 to report on a remedy. His plan recommended digging extensive "catchwater" drains to surround the fens allowing water to be diverted away from them and he also devised a system of smaller channels to actually drain the land. The cost was to be £600,000 and this meant 14,000 acres of the "new" land being sold off to entrepreneurs to raise the necessary funds. Parliament passed an enabling Act in 1801 and the work took until 1813 to complete. Rennie's scheme resulted in the creation of the West Fen Drain and the East and West Fen Catchwater Drains, which combine to form the Stonebridge Drain, and it is these waterways that now form the bulk of the "Navigable Drains" meeting at Cowbridge.

From the outset the drains were also used by boats to transport crops, especially cereals, grown on the huge area of newly available farmland and by the 1850s there were 14 regular packet boats known to be travelling to Bargate Bridge, Boston from as far afield as Revesby and Hagnaby bringing people to markets; indeed such boat services continued into the early 20th century.

In the early days of regular postal services there was often no individual delivery with mail simply being left in bulk at agreed distribution points. An unusual feature at Cowbridge, now sadly gone, was the pole on which a flag was flown to tell the locals that mail was awaiting collection.

The railway, crossed twice on the walk, is the former East Lincolnshire main line built by the Great Northern Railway. It opened southwards from Grimsby in stages from March 1848 reaching Boston in October and being fully open to Peterborough two weeks after that. It was a busy freight line carrying enormous quantities of Grimsby fish and Lincolnshire potatoes to London. Many small stations were closed in September 1961 although the line remained operational until 1970. It is now open only between Boston and Firsby South Curve where it joins what was previously a separate Firsby to Skegness branch line.

Boston Golf Club has had several homes since it was founded in 1900 but came to its present site at Cowbridge in 1962. Its beautiful landscaping can be enjoyed from the public rights of way that cross it and it has had the honour of being described in the *Boston Standard* by the town's Preservation Trust as a "delight to the eye". The drains also encourage a variety of wildfowl and along the tree-lined Cowbridge Drain it is worth watching out for kingfishers.

NOTES. There is verge-side parking in the lane approaching Boston Golf Club; turn into it after crossing Richardson's Bridge. Please park considerately. Take care on the two road sections. On the (very) short B1183 section it's worth crossing to the pavement.

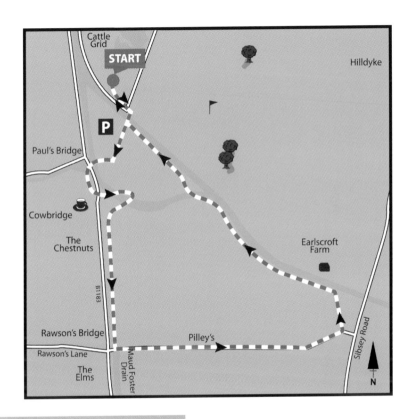

ABOUT THE WALK

START : Near the
Golf Course entrance.
(GR328475)

MAPS : OS Landranger 131
: Explorer 261.

DISTANCE : 2.5 miles :
4 kilometres.

REFRESHMENTS : Cowbridge
House Inn.

1 Initially proceed towards the
golf club entrance and bear right at
the footpath signpost just before the
clubhouse access bridge. At the next
signpost (a three-way one) keep forward
with the Stone Bridge Drain now on
your left. At a junction with the Maud
Foster Drain bear right to the lock and
cross over it to the road. Walk left for 80
yards until level with an iron footbridge
and turn left to cross that too. (Note the
information board near the small nearby
parking area.)

Walk 16

② Walk ahead for a few yards before bearing right to pass round a garden onto a track and follow that alongside the Maud Foster Drain to a bridle gate at Rawson's Bridge and join a road (Pilleys Lane). Turn left over the railway and continue until you reach a bend and "T" junction just before the main road. Turn left and in a few yards left again onto a track. (No footpath sign!)

③ Follow this grassy track, now beside the Cowbridge Drain, and eventually re-cross the railway; then in a further 75 yards look for a footpath sign pointing to the right. Turn off and descend the grass bank in front of you so that you pass between a sealed off drain (with a ruined lock on your left) and the main Cowbridge Drain.

④ Simply walk ahead now on the lower, mown flood bank to a bridge. Cross this to the three-way footpath you passed earlier and turn right to head back to the start.

Birth of a Victorian Spa

Woodhall Spa, Coal Pit Woods and
the Wellington Monument

This walk explores the woodlands closely associated with
the town's historical origins, but also visits an unusual and
intriguing Napoleonic War monument. We return along the
closed Horncastle branch railway, now part of the Viking Way.

Woodhall seems an unlikely place for a colliery but discovering coal was the dream of entrepreneur John Parkinson when he sank shafts there in the early 1800s. He spent two years, and much money, sinking a ten foot wide shaft some thousand or so feet deep trying to find coal and there are apocryphal tales of miners, intent on prolonging their jobs, who smuggled in small pieces of coal which they could conveniently "find" as evidence of progress. Geological problems and flooding led to Parkinson's eventual failure. The episode is however still recalled at Coal Pit Wood behind the present day Teahouse in the Woods (now Macauley's Restaurant) and a mineshaft

is still depicted on the town sign in Stixwould Road.

Parkinson's activities had unintended results and led indirectly to Woodhall becoming a "Spa". The abandoned shafts filled with water, which soon became recognized by locals as having remarkable healing properties, not only for themselves but also for their cattle. In the 1840s Squire Thomas Hotchkin had a sample analysed only to discover concentrations of bromine and iodine higher than any other known spa water. Woodhall's future prosperity was then ensured, though the spa's full potential was not realised until the railway arrived;

this anticipated "potential" being a major factor in securing promoting of the railway in the first place. So in 1855 the Kirkstead Junction Railway Company opened their Horncastle branch line following which event the town's popularity soon became international and lasted until after World War I. The railway remained even then, not closing until 1954. The final economic blow to Woodhall came on September 21, 1983 when the wells unexpectedly collapsed; they have not been used since, although there are plans to try and re-open them. The walk passes the abandoned Spa Pump Rooms.

The walk also passes around the grounds of the Petwood Hotel. During World War II Woodhall had its own airfield, to the south towards Tattershall, and the Petwood Hotel became the base for the Dambusters. Their impressive memorial can be seen in the Royal Gardens, Woodhall where once stood the Royal Hotel, destroyed by bombing in August 1943. The huge memorial is appropriately shaped as a symbolic broken dam with waters flooding through.

We will also visit the "Waterloo Wood" just to the north of the village that commemorates victory in an earlier European conflict. The acorns that grew into the woodland here were planted in 1815, soon after Wellington's famous victory during the Napoleonic Wars.

At that time national military heroes generated immense popularity, and this was especially true of such victors as Admiral Nelson and the Duke of Wellington. The 36-feet-high monument to Wellington did not appear until 1844 and it was the brainchild of Colonel Richard Elmhirst from nearby Stixwould (who had been at Waterloo with Wellington) and whose initials are carved beside the somewhat wordy inscription. Note that Wellington himself does not look across to "greet" you – his visitors – but off at a tangent. Directly towards Waterloo in Belgium in fact!

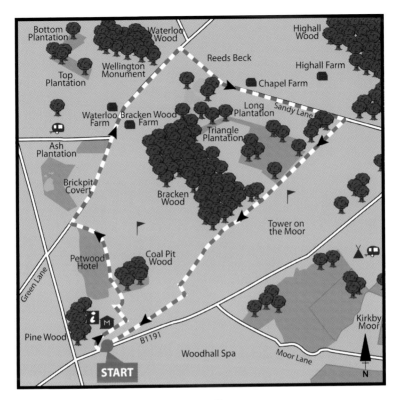

START : Broadway car park, Woodhall Spa.

MAPS : OS Landranger 122 : Explorer 273.

DISTANCE : 4.3 miles : 7 kilometres.

REFRESHMENTS : Woodhall Spa has numerous places of refreshment.

1 Leave the car park and turn right, doubling sharply right again almost at once into Spa Road. Pass George Avenue before turning left and reaching a footpath sign outside the Teahouse in the Woods (Macauley's). If you walk a few yards beyond the restaurant you will get a front view of the old spa buildings, now very dilapidated, and see the famous Kinema. This began life as an Edwardian tennis pavilion but has been a cinema since 1922. It is unique in having the only working back projection system in the country and is decorated inside with unusual eye-tricking wall murals.

2 Follow the footpath as it curves left to pass behind the restaurant and the ruins of the Spa buildings, within which are the collapsed mineral wells. The path is now easy to follow past Coalpit Wood and around the perimeter of the Petwood Hotel grounds to reach a road beside the golf course.

3 Turn right, and keep walking ahead at a "T" junction. After a mile you will reach Waterloo Wood and the Wellington Monument can be seen on your left. A little further on turn right again into Sandy Lane, continuing for a further mile to a kissing gate and waymarked

footpath on the right. Here we join the Viking Way and you will see the distinctive helmet logo waymark.

4 Follow the path over the golf course, keeping a watch for flying golf balls! When you reach the Manor House go left only for a few feet, then turn right along the old railway. This will lead you back to the car park at the start.

5 You can finish the walk by continuing along Station Road to the Royal Gardens and visit the Dambusters memorial.

Unexpected 20th Century Industrial Heritage

Nettleton and the Ironstone Mines

For this walk we travel to Nettleton in the northern Wol
to savour the splendid views from Nettleton Hill. We als
explore the Nettleton Valley, an area known locally as "
Switzerland", which conceals the remains of a surprising
former industry.

To find the start leave the A46 at Nettleton and drive through the village onto the Normanby-Le-Wold road. As this starts to climb steeply the ramblers' car park is on your right.

Nettleton is an important centre for ramblers being at the junction of two long distance footpaths. The Viking Way passes through on its way south and the village is also the finish point of a 57-mile-long route commemorating one of Lincolnshire's most charismatic ramblers. The "Nev Cole Way", begins at Burton Stather and follows the Humber bank before crossing the Wolds to end at Nettleton. It was inaugurated after his death in 1989 by the Wanderlust

Ramblers of Grimsby, of which he was a founder member in the 1930s, to commemorate his life-long defence of ramblers' rights. We shall climb his memorial stile on this walk.

Nettleton, surrounded by hills, has Lincolnshire's highest ground nearby at the trigonometric point just beyond Nettleton Top (GR121965) and we pass close to this before descending into the Nettleton Valley. There is geological interest too for these hills contain strata of rare red chalk and thick seams of "Claxby Ironstone", so named because it was first mined during the 1880s in the nearby village of that name. Mining soon began at Nettleton too, though in a small way at first. From 1929 a significant industry developed, employing nearly 200 men as railway tunnels were driven through the western ridge of the Nettleton Valley to reach the seams on the eastern side. Maximum output came in 1967 when 277,700 tons of ore were produced. However the ore had a low iron content and foreign imports eventually became more economical, leading to the mines being closed in 1969. Traces of the old tunnels are seen beside the walk but otherwise few visible scars remain of this industrial past. The splendid scenery now plays a recreational role for walkers on the Viking Way; a section of which we follow from Nettleton Top.

In Nettleton itself the rough stone tower of St. John the Baptist church was built from the local ironstone with its rich,

golden-reddish colour but which, because of its softness, reveals its susceptibility to weather erosion. The oldest part of the tower is Saxon, the upper parts having been rebuilt in 1874. The lovely clock is noteworthy for having been made in 1837 by James Harrison, grandson of John Harrison - of *Longitude* fame - who came from Barrow-on-Humber.

NOTES. This is a strenuous walk; parts being rough and steep underfoot. Two described short cuts (2½ miles or 4¾ miles) avoid the long valley descent (see route directions). Those with picnics should opt for the viewpoint of Nettleton Hill or somewhere in the valley. Some permissive paths are used on Nettleton Hill and these do not appear on OS maps.

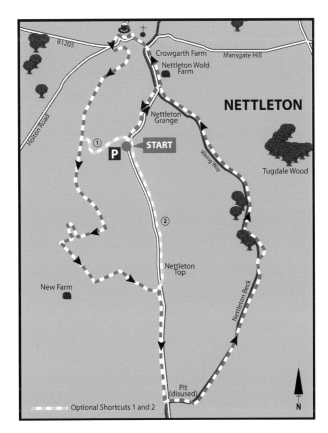

START : Ramblers' car park, Nettleton. (GR111993)

MAPS : OS Landranger 113 (Grimsby) : Explorer 284.

DISTANCE : 6.8 miles : 11 kilometres.

REFRESHMENTS : Salutation Inn Nettleton. Inns, shops and cafés in Caistor.

① From the car park turn left and walk back through Nettleton village past the church to the A46 by the Salutation Inn and turn left. Opposite the Moortown Road junction look on your left for an access map for the permissive path onto Nettleton Hill. Double back left to walk behind the hedge before swinging right uphill to a stile. Marker posts indicate the continuing route uphill to a final post on the skyline near a hedge corner. Go left around this to walk along the ridge top with magnificent views, especially to the

west where, on very clear days, the Derbyshire Pennines are visible. Continue to a stile and another access map. [The first short cut keeps left of the fence here; then descending left puts you onto a downhill track that emerges near the car park.]

② Otherwise climb the stile and walk along the hilltop with a fence/hedge on your left until at a hedge corner you must turn right downhill. Turn right again by the bottom hedge for about 120 yards, then climb the stile to your left and double back behind the hedge onto a public right of way. Continue following waymarks along field edges for half a mile to a surfaced lane; the remnants of an old mine road. Turn left uphill, swinging right where the surface worsens until you join the Nettleton/Normanby road. [Turn left here for the second short cut, which is all on the road, back to the start.]

③ To continue the full walk turn right. In about half a mile, just before Acre House turn left onto the Viking Way waymarked with the Viking "Helmet" logo. After going through a gate bear left down the valley, (with wonderful views again!) but be sure to veer across to a stile in the hedge on the opposite slope.

The way is now clear down to a point near an old tunnel entrance from where a waymarked detour goes round old mine entrances. Beyond these continue down the valley past a lake towards Nettleton. When a track joins from the right bear left to climb the Neville Cole Memorial stile onto a track to walk past a farm. On reaching the road turn left and head back to the start.

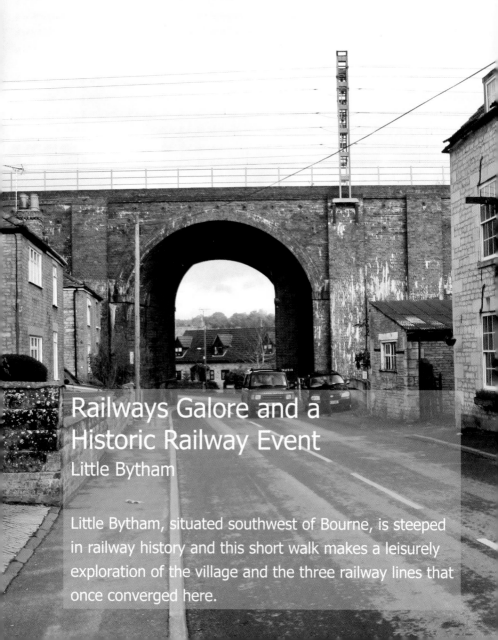

Railways Galore and a Historic Railway Event
Little Bytham

Little Bytham, situated southwest of Bourne, is steeped
in railway history and this short walk makes a leisurely
exploration of the village and the three railway lines that
once converged here.

All this railway history is combined with a gentle walk by the Glen Brook and in meadows by the West Glen River, both of which have picturesque fords.

Nowhere else in Lincolnshire has such a small village been so dominated by railways as Little Bytham. This legacy survives today in the form of an enormous viaduct that still carries the main line between London and

Line", which ran through Grantham, was opened and it was this line that passed above Little Bytham. A beautifully painted pub sign (a real work of art!) depicting Sir Nigel Gresley's locomotive "Mallard", once adorned the inn here. The significance of the inn's name in this location is due to the fact that Mallard achieved the world steam locomotive

Scotland. The viaduct soars high above the main street with the cottages and the former "The Mallard" inn huddled beside the arches. The original Great Northern Railway main line to the north of England (the Lincolnshire "Loop Line") ran from Peterborough via Boston and Lincoln. However, in 1852 the "Towns

speed record of 125 mph on July 3, 1938 whilst running on the line south from Grantham.

Just south of the village, and passing under this main line, are the disused embankments and bridges of a second railway, that of the Midland and Great

Northern Joint Railway (MGNJR). This line was in operation between 1894 and 1959, providing a link from Leicester, through Bourne, to Kings Lynn and Norfolk.

Finally, and with more local interest, there was the Edenham Branch Railway, privately built and operated by Lord Willoughby de Eresby of nearby Grimsthorpe Castle. This opened in 1855 and closed in 1873 and ran from Edenham, four miles away on the far side of Grimsthorpe Park, to Little Bytham. The track curved downhill to terminate alongside the GNR main line half a mile south of the village. During the construction and operation of his railway Lord Willoughby sought expert advice from one of Britain's greatest railway engineers, Daniel Gooch, famously associated with the Great Western Railway. Early in his career another great name in British railway history, William Stroudley of the London, Brighton and South Coast Railway, was an engine driver for Lord Willoughby. All three lines are clearly traceable on the OS maps.

Little Bytham itself is an attractive village of old stone houses, and anyone interested in churches will enjoy visiting St. Medards, which has a very rare dedication to a 6th century French bishop. There is Norman stonework both on the tower and inside the church and there is also an exceptionally fine carved

priest's door on the south side.

NOTES. Parking in the village is limited so please be considerate to residents and other road users. Where the walk follows roads (albeit quiet ones) use pavements where you can. A shorter route is suggested in the route directions! The only inn nearby is the "Willoughby Arms" about half a mile south towards Careby.

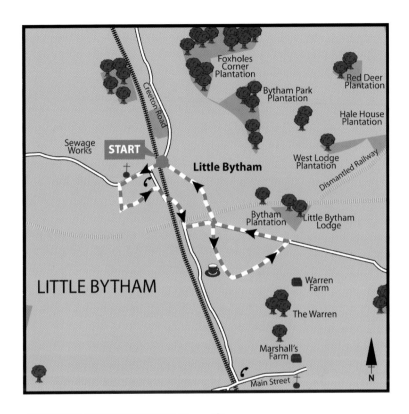

START : Near the railway
viaduct in Little Bytham village.

MAPS : OS Landranger sheet
130 (Grantham) : Explorer 248.

DISTANCE : 2.5 miles :
4 kilometres.

REFRESHMENTS : Willoughby
Arms, Little Bytham.

1 Set off with your back to the viaduct
and walk past the road junction and the
church. In a further 200 yards turn left
down the lane by the Old Rectory and
cross the Glen Brook at the footbridge
by a ford. Now turn left again, being
careful to stay by the stream when the
track veers right. You will soon reach
another ford; from this keep ahead
down a surfaced lane. At the road turn
right, walking out of the village by
passing under both the main line and the
abandoned MGNJR railway.

At a "T" junction turn left for 200 yards to reach two footpath signs on opposite sides of the road. The short route turns left here, but note that only from the longer route is anything seen of Lord Willoughby's railway. (To follow the short route turn left and go to (*) below.) Otherwise turn right.

You are now walking beside the West Glen River. Near a tumbledown bridge, which once carried the Edenham branch, the path goes sharply left and gradually climbs alongside the old embankment. As you walk along this section of the route you may also have the opportunity to see deer as they reside in the vicinity. In a quarter of a mile, near trees, the path curves left to

join the road. This road crosses the old Edenham branch on an original brick bridge 150 yards to your right. Use the road to return downhill to the two footpath signs you passed earlier and turn right.

(*) In a few yards the path passes under the former MGNJR line on a walkway cantilevered out under a bridge. (Dark, echoey and exciting for children – and perhaps for some adults too!) Continue to a kissing gate and a stile near some telegraph poles. Now veer left across a large meadow gradually converging with the river again. Near the far left hand corner is a stile. Climb over, turn left to re-cross the river and walk back into the village through the railway viaduct.

Walk 20

From the Romans to World War II

Martin, Metheringham Airfield and the Car Dyke

This easy walk offers contrasting ancient and modern history as we visit both the Roman Car Dyke and Metheringham WWII airfield; our main points of interest.

Martin, the "village by the marsh", lies about four miles southwest of Woodhall Spa and is aptly named for its situation beside the Witham Fens. Little local history is known before the Romans built their 56-mile-long Car Dyke linking the River Nene to the River Witham near Lincoln. This passes close to the village but even after much investigation and debate archaeologists remain uncertain as to its true purpose though it probably acted as both a drainage system and a supply route, using the Fossdyke, the Trent and the Ouse to reach York. Either way it was skilfully surveyed along what modern maps show as the

25 feet contour line with the excavated earth used to form banks containing a watercourse up to 30 feet wide. We walk beside one of the best preserved sections where a variety of water plants and birds can be seen; where trees overhang the riverbanks keep a watch for kingfishers.

To the northwest of Martin lies Metheringham Airfield. Astonishingly when construction was to begin in 1942 local farmers were given only 48 hours notice to vacate their land. RAF Metheringham opened in October 1943 and 106 Squadron were the first to arrive with only a week to prepare for action. By the armistice this squadron had lost 187 aircraft but gained 267 medals! The airfield was unusual too in being one of only four in Lincolnshire to use FIDO (Fog Intensive Dispersal Operation), a system of pipes beside the runways through which 1,500 gallons of petrol could be pumped and burnt every minute, the intense rising heat helping to evaporate fog! Metheringham's usefulness ended once peace was declared and it finally closed in 1946.

We will cross part of the airfield to see the 106 Squadron Memorial. Nearby at Westmoor Farm, just west of the B1189 (GR103596) is an Airfield Visitor Centre with fascinating displays of memorabilia. It is well worth a visit. (Please call telephone number: (01526) 378 270 to check on opening times.)

Some cultural elements along our walk come in the form of sculptures commissioned by North Kesteven DC as part of a scheme to introduce art into the countryside. By the Car Dyke are two carvings in oak by Steve Gelliot. The first sculpture is an unusual seat representing the "Exchange of Elements", an allusion to the changes wrought by local fen drainage – that is, water to soil, which produces crops and seed, which in turn becomes food. Further on a large wooden "medallion" recalls the local Roman presence. Finally, near the start of our walk there is a colourful mosaic by Arik Haflon depicting a Roman surveyor complete with theodolite looking towards the distant Car Dyke.

NOTES. The car park was unsigned on my visit, but when approaching from Woodhall Spa look over to the left, opposite the road junction just before Martin village. A shorter 4 mile walking option is also offered. Tiny bits of the route are on Explorer sheets 272 and 261; although walkers will easily be able to manage without them!

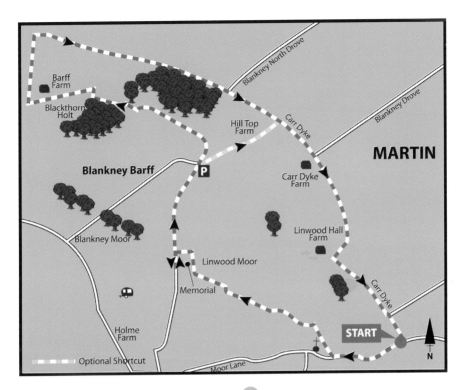

ABOUT THE WALK

START : "Stepping Out" car park at Martin (GR128600).

MAPS : OS Landranger 121 (Lincoln) : Explorer 273.

DISTANCE : 5.6 miles : 9 kilometres.

REFRESHMENTS : Royal Oak, Martin. Holmdale House Tearooms, Martin.

1 Walk first into Martin village and beyond the Royal Oak and the chapel, turn right into Mill Lane and go left through a hedge at a footpath sign. Follow the field edge to the corner and then turn left and join another lane (Linwood Road). Turn right and then immediately left onto North Moor Lane, which becomes a grass track leading to a barn, before finally narrowing to a path by trees. After a footbridge turn left onto a farm track to reach the old airfield. You need to turn right shortly, but first head left a few paces for the 106 Squadron Memorial. Return to the track and walk

along the airfield to a road junction. [The short route bears right here along the road towards Blankney Fen and reaches the Car Dyke in a quarter of a mile. Join the main route by turning right.]

② Otherwise cross to a red metal barrier by another memorial, continuing along the airfield perimeter road as it bears left. When it bends left a second time turn off to the right onto a

grass track and from a waymark follow the footpath running between woods and a fence. At a farm track go right, then almost immediately left, to reach a junction near Metheringham Barff Farm. Now turn right past the farm to arrive at the Car Dyke, cross it and turn right along a concrete road. Just after Delph End Farm is the carved seat, below to your left.

③ At a public road keep walking forward until the road bends left, then continue past cottages along a gravel track and later on grass. By the second gate and stile look left for the next sculpture. From a third gate and a stile cross a track, go over another stile and bear right in a long "L" shaped meadow. Bearing left at the angle, climb another stile and continue beside the Car Dyke. At the next road keep walking ahead back towards the mosaic sculpture and the start of our walk.

127